EATING MYSELF CRAZY

HOW I MADE PEACE WITH FOOD
(AND HOW YOU CAN TOO)

BY TREENA WYNES

indie ink
PUBLISHING

Cover & book design: Jacqueline Germin (jgermin.com)
Cover & author photo: Jamie Lawrence (capturedsoulsphotography.com)
Back cover author photo: Martine Sansoucy (martinesansoucy.co.nr)
Editor: Jen Pederson

Eating myself crazy: how I made peace with food and how you can too
©2013 by Treena Wynes

Published by Indie Ink Publishing
#220, 220 20th Street West
Saskatoon, SK, Canada   S7M 0W9
T: 888.438.1343

Printed in Canada by Friesens Book Division
First edition: March, 2013

ISBN: 978-0-9878105-6-4

Library and Archives Canada Cataloguing in Publication

Wynes, Treena
Eating myself crazy: how I made peace with food and how you can too/Treena Wynes.

Includes bibliographical references and index.
Issued also in an electronic format.

1. Wynes, Treena–Health. 2. Eating disorders–Patients–Biography.
3. Eating disorders–Psychological aspects. 4. Eating disorders–Treatment. I. Title.

RC552.E18W96 2013   616.85'26   C2012-907702-X

I would like to dedicate this book to my two boys, Spencer and Chase, who are so well-mannered, responsible and independent, allowing me to concentrate on writing this book. I am honored to be your mother.

Acknowledgements

I would like to give my thanks and appreciation to those who supported me in bringing this book to reality. I owe a huge debt of gratitude to my husband and sons for adapting to a new lifestyle and for putting up with the fact that certain foods never cross our threshold anymore. Also for taking on some of my household responsibilities so I could sit down and write this book. Chase, my boy, you have become the most excellent cook!

I wish to thank my friends and colleagues for their tremendous response and encouragement toward my goal to educate others about foods and moods. I am grateful for receiving numerous emails on new research or news articles related to my message providing me the momentum to keep talking and writing.

I am also extremely grateful to my publisher, Suzanne, of Indie Ink Publishing, for taking a chance on me and guiding me through this exciting process. You carry such a passion that can sweep anyone into your domain of imagery and vision.

I could have never written this book without all the remarkable people in my life. I am truly fortunate to have such a large circle of supporters near and far blessing me with their inspirational words.

TABLE OF CONTENTS

CHAPTER 1
MIND + EMOTIONS = BEHAVIORS

CHAPTER 2

FEED YOUR MOODS, CHANGE YOUR BODY

CHAPTER 3

RECIPES FOR LIFE

Note from the author

That's me on the front cover. It shows how I felt for most of my life around food. I'm sure many of you can relate to this picture, but, as a counselor I also know that it is your unique set of traits, history and complex issues that drive you to eat (or to not eat). My story may have similarities to yours but it will be different. There are as many stories as there are individuals. That's why it's important to reveal and then truly examine the reasons behind your emotional eating.

Food was my coping mechanism when I felt drained, bored or upset. Wanting comfort and pleasure and getting it from food caused me to repeat my behavior, but it seemed I could never eat enough to be truly satisfied. In fact, the first bite would stimulate the urge even more, throwing me completely out of control. The guilt and shame associated with compulsive eating was demoralizing and brutal on my self-esteem.

Using food to cope is an easy, pleasant and accessible method to deal with a really bad day. In fact, it doesn't even have to be a "bad" day. It can just be a hurried, hectic day that begs for that soft, mushy carb-y food to bring your tight shoulders down from your ears. But the more we use food to calm our nerves, ease our pain, or get through those low energy days, the more we become reliant on it. The consequences will eventually show up on our waistlines, spurring the panic diet, where we swear off all kinds of foods. As many have experienced, this doesn't work. Why? Because it doesn't address our emotional dependency on food.

The hardest part of conquering emotional eating is letting go of our justifications for our unwanted behavior. I've had several "this-is-my-last-time" moments only to feel like absolute crap after I did what I had hoped I wouldn't do. Obstacles and life challenges will never go away and there may never be that right time to start a new behavior or make changes. Our warped relationship with food, our obsession with body image and our chronic bombardment by numerous stressors are causing us to eat ourselves crazy.

In this book, I share with you my story of anguish, confusion and triumph over food. I provide you some relevant information that is not readily available to the general public. And I share with you some simple strategies and tools that worked for me. I hope this may help you on your path to recovery from emotional eating. This book is not to be a replacement for appropriate medical advice, attention or treatment. However, my objective is to introduce the idea that we all have our own natural solutions hidden inside of us.

My hope is that this book will help awaken your senses, shake up some of your notions of food and dieting and give you strength and confidence to overcome your emotional eating.

Treena Wynes, *BSW, RSW*

How to use this book effectively

This book is set up in a specific way to help you be successful in your wellness goals, whether they are losing weight, preventing illnesses, enhancing moods, or providing better nutrition to your family. The good news is that whatever forward steps you make towards healthier eating habits, you will be preventing illness and diseases.

Most people will feel inclined to jump in and just follow the eating plan provided. However, there are only a few options given for those who may not know where to start. If you read the information provided first then you will understand why it's important to eliminate some foods and increase others. The eating plan is not designed to be restricting, as taking small progressive steps will ensure more success than the all-or-nothing approach.

Preparation and planning are keys to a good start. Stocking up on supplies is important, as it saves you from having to run out and pick up ingredients. Many of the food items are easily found in your grocery store; however, some items may only be available at your local health food store. More good news: Many large grocery chains are beginning to recognize the trend of organic, whole and local foods and incorporating them into their stores.

Self-awareness is also a major part of weight-loss efforts. The journaling built into this book is not to make you feel guilty or bad if you choose to eat foods you know are counterproductive to your goals. It's important for you to take notice of the times you crave certain foods and whether those times are linked to certain events of the day. There's no need to rationalize why you ate this or that, but to be aware that certain events trigger you. Patience and gentle honesty toward yourself will reap more rewards than self-criticism and negative thoughts. You are what you think. Self-talk should be no different than the way you would encourage a co-worker, friend or child.

After you read the book thoroughly, decide on mini-goals first such as adding more fruits and vegetables to your daily diet. The focus for the first month should be on eliminating some foods and incorporating some healthier foods. Weaning yourself from sweets or fast foods will be a difficult task and will bring on withdrawals if you're addicted to sugar and additives. Self-care and other coping strategies need to be planned for the first month.

Reading this book over and over will also ensure that the information is ingrained. Repetition creates habits. Also, start studying other information in books, magazines, the Internet and videos that will assist in reminders of your wellness goals. Two excellent websites are *mercola.com* and *drhyman.com*.

The recipes provided are easy and will open the door for you to start introducing more homemade meals to your diet. Cooking can be quick and easy once you realize different shortcuts that work for you. Check out *Food4Thought* tidbits to learn a few tricks to get more nutrition into your diet faster and easier and let your inner chef get creative.

Remember—this is not a quick fix. It may take four to six months to achieve dramatic results. The more diligent you are on your mini-goals, the more permanent the benefits. Focusing on a small specific goal will increase the success of changing an unwanted habit. You will be farther ahead than you were last year and the year before that. Be proud of your accomplishments no matter how small!

My story—"Hey, Fatty!"

There were two incidents that quickly educated me that there was a standard in body shape that I apparently was not following. To make matters worse, I wasn't told nicely. I was berated in front of others.

My first experience learning the importance of body image came at five years old—the day of Kindergarten school pictures. My mom had brushed out my shiny strawberry blonde hair and put me in a red turtleneck. I was so excited to get my first school picture taken. The assembling of the students was a bit disorganized. The library filled as a few classrooms of students at a time piled into where the pictures were being taken. It was fairly cramped and I was trying to stay near my class, but was shoved off to the side by some older kids who said, "Get out of the way, Fatty."

I was stunned and hurt and stopped in my tracks. Others continued to push me further from my class. I started to panic because I was getting lost in the mayhem and could see through a small opening of kids that my class was getting its picture taken. I desperately pushed my way to the staffroom where I knew my mom was visiting. I started crying to my mom that I was pushed and was missing having my picture taken. With that, she took my hand and barged right through the crowd. She put me right front of the camera, wiped my tears, gave me a kiss and told me to smile a big smile. I sat in front of the camera with the big bright light shining in my face feeling like I was on display for all to see. I squeezed out the best smile I could, but inside my heart was sinking.

The second experience was in my first gymnastics class a couple weeks later. I was so excited to start my class as I loved to do somersaults and tumble around. My mom recognized this and thought it was the perfect activity for me. I was so proud of the gymnastics outfit my mom bought me. It was a red jumpsuit with red tights and little slippers. I felt like a ballerina and was eagerly prancing around in it. Just before the classes started I went in the dressing room with a couple of the kids I knew. We ran into two girls who were about three years older than us. They focused their attention on me, looking me up and down. They started pointing and laughing at me. "You look like a big, fat, red tomato!" They kept laughing and walked away.

A huge lump formed in my throat and tears welled up. I wanted to run as far away from there as fast as I could. I never went back. My mother couldn't understand why, given that all I did was somersault after somersault at home. I didn't tell her due to my embarrassment and worry she would call their parents (or worse) speak to them directly. My shame over my body shape was preventing me from doing something I loved. I quickly went from a happy-go-lucky little girl to one who felt she wasn't the same as everyone else. I started feeling shame about my body size, feeling others were constantly scrutinizing my appearance.

Lots to learn

At five years old, I had no awareness of my body image or that I was fat until I was told so. Even my idea of "fat" wasn't clear or accurate, as my only comparison with fat people was Santa Claus. I certainly couldn't look like Santa Claus, could I? I started to become self-conscious about my body and was insecure and shy around kids older than me. Luckily, over the next couple of years I lost my baby fat and didn't hear much about it until my teen years, but the thoughts of being fat remained.

Knowing what I know now, three things come to mind when I think of those two significant moments. First, it clearly shows how very early childhood social experiences can quickly mold one's self-image and self-esteem. Second, it shows that experiences, combined with strong, intense negative emotions have the ability to bore a hole in your mind and influence your thoughts for a long time. And third: What was my mom thinking dressing a chubby kid in tight red clothing?!?

Seriously, we can all relate to times when we received negative feedback and it may have taken us totally off guard. Depending on the power you give it, it can totally change your view of yourself. As a child, your self-esteem is forming and your self-concept is being influenced by the immediate environment and other people's feedback. My self-esteem had started on shaky ground and I was now hypersensitive to other people's judgments. I now couldn't trust my own self-concept because it obviously was so off the mark from how other people seemed to see me.

As I long as I was willing to give the power to other people, my inability to trust myself was going to make my life very difficult.

Comfort food discovered

The summer I turned 14 years old, my family and I moved to another town. Everything I knew and cherished was left behind—My best friend, my grandparents, my school and (most of all) my house in front of the lake where I spent most of my childhood playing. It became a very depressing summer for me. No lake, no friends…no happiness. I spent most of it hidden in a new, unfamiliar house and didn't dare venture outside in case someone saw me. I didn't get much sunshine or exercise, which was out of character—normally I loved running around in summer shorts and bare feet in the summer heat. That summer I just stayed in my room reading or watching TV in the family room.

My mom took to baking every day and made fresh bread, buns and (best of all) cinnamon buns. She made the big, sticky ones the size of my dad's hand where you had to lick the sweet cinnamon syrup off your fingers. It was the only thing that brightened my lonely days. I had at least three or four a day. This is when my love for bread and sugar flourished and became my favorite comfort food. The smell of fresh bread warmed my heart and the taste filled my emptiness and distracted me from boredom. I was also dreading starting at a new school, and the freshly baked dough felt like a fuzzy blanket wrapped around me, giving me the sense that everything was going to be all right.

After meeting some new friends and starting school, things became much better. I seemed to have been accepted easily and everything became new and exciting. After school I came home to freshly baked bread and scarfed down two thick pieces with lots of peanut butter and milk. I noticed after awhile that my pants were getting a little tighter and I needed new ones. It didn't really bother me until months later when my childhood best friend told me that she received my new school picture I mailed. She said she showed it to my old classmates who were shocked to see how much weight I gained.

What she said was like a slap in the face, more like a wake-up slap, as I wasn't aware it was so noticeable to others. The feelings from Kindergarten came back to me in a rush. I immediately swore off my mom's baking. I would lose whatever weight I had gained because being fat was not going to make me popular among my new classmates. The realization that I was fatter than I thought and that, again, I had not been aware of my body size threw me in a panic to lose weight.

Dieting for a 14-year-old was all about calorie restriction as that was the only knowledge I had about losing weight. I scrutinized my food and restricted the ones that were high calorie or known to have fat in them. For months I tried not eat any bread or cinnamon buns but the cravings were so persistent that eventually I would cave, tearing into a thick slice of bread or a cinnamon bun and then agonize over how I was going to deal with the calories.

I exercised to music in my room hoping to burn the calories off, which seemed to help somewhat. I weighed myself twice a day, once in the morning to see if I lost any weight and again after school to determine how much I would allow myself to eat. When I didn't have any bread or sugar the cravings would be so intense that I would resort to eating a bowl of cereal or a handful of chocolate chips in an attempt to suppress the cravings. It never really completely satisfied me, but it helped take the edge off.

The next trick I used to try to motivate myself was to post pictures of models from my pile of fashion magazines all over my room. I would regularly compare myself to them especially, in regard to the stomach area. Their waistlines and stomachs were flawless, smooth and sexy. I had bumps and folds that would spill over from my jeans. I would feel disgusting and gross after looking at these pictures but it was the self-torture I needed to get myself to stop eating.

I rode this crazy train of calorie-in, calorie-out for about a year and after many failed attempts to control my eating I needed another way of dealing with my fluctuating weight and over-eating. Eliminating bread, sugar and fat was a daily battle and one that I wasn't winning. I was starting to eat out a lot with my friends. Hamburgers, fries, chicken fingers, and pizza were almost a daily occurrence and I could see the number on the scale starting to creep up. I desperately needed a solution. My body image was becoming more and more important: girls my age were hooking up with boyfriends, and I had one in my sight. However, the boy I liked had the attention of another girl who was much skinnier in my mind. Food was ruining everything for me.

The last resort

I had heard one of my friends joking around about people forcing themselves to throw up after eating. It may have been a toss away comment, but I zeroed in on it. That's it, I thought. This is the solution to my problem! Would I actually have the guts to do it? I decided I had to; there was no other way. A couple of days later when nobody else was home, I gave it a try. It wasn't as easy as I thought it would be. There was a lot of gagging, choking and "God, this is disgusting," with only a bit of food coming up. My eyes watered and my face was red from holding my breath. I tried a couple of more times until I finally figured out where exactly my fingers had to be in my throat, and it all come up. I finally had my "get-out-of-jail-free" card.

Becoming a bulimic wasn't something I planned to do. I thought that purging was only going to be an option when I was desperate; a last resort when my eating got out of control and I overate. I thought I would be able to maintain my "diet" (whatever that was) and keep my eating under control. That ended up not being the case—not at all. My dependency on food to feel good and comfort me on the bad days was going against my diet ideals which led me to the bathroom over and over. It was a vicious and painful circle.

Purging was easier than controlling my food. The first bite would trigger all my senses and draw me into an eating frenzy. Everything was starting to get more and more out of control and so was my behavior. My moods were all over the place which resulted in more eating. I was also starting to experiment with drinking on weekends, adding to more out of control behavior. My closet was stashed with chips, sugary cereals and candy with a lock on my door to ensure no one would see and eat it. I couldn't concentrate in class and my marks were starting to plummet in Grade 10. I was skipping breakfast to save calories only to end up giving in to the intense cravings of sugar and fat at the end of the day. The end of the day usually resulted in purging and feeling terrible for doing so.

The shame of my eating disorder was the worst part. I would absolutely die if anyone found out. I always made sure there were cleaning supplies in the bathroom cabinet to clean the toilet or for anything that missed its target. When my family was around, I would say that I was going to have a quick bath or shower to cover my gagging and the contents splashing into the bowl. I figured out how to throw up as quietly as possible. I learned that ice cream was quiet, easy on the throat and made things come up nicely so I always had a bowl of ice cream at the end of dinner. There were so many tricks needed. Keeping my bulimia a secret was the ultimate goal.

My mother noticed my preoccupation with dieting and losing weight. She was concerned that I wasn't eating. One day she found my undigested contents in the bowl and confronted me about it. I can't remember the lie I made up but I knew she didn't buy it. It cost me a trip to a social worker. I didn't want to go and protested, but there I was, being questioned about my feelings about my body and food in the social worker's office. I told the social worker that it was the first time I tried it and I hated it. That it was gross and hurt my throat and I would never do it again. I explained I must have forgotten to flush the toilet because I immediately wanted to get the taste off my breath by brushing my teeth. The social worker bought it and I never had to see her again.

I don't remember the exact details but I remember being so angry with mother and writing her a letter saying that she was trying to ruin my life by making me fat. I left her the note on my parents' bed and didn't come home that night in retaliation. When I returned she was more upset about me going A.W.O.L. than the accusation of trying to make me fat. She said it was a ridiculous comment and that she was just worried about my disturbing eating habits.

My bulimia was up and down and went on for several months after this incident. There were times when it was twice a day and times when I wouldn't throw up for a week. There was one period when I actually thought I was on the way to recovery. In Grade 12, I was eating healthier and working out regularly. My marks were starting to come up and my head felt clearer. I didn't have the symptoms I had previously with purging such as headaches, chronic tonsillitis, mood swings, constant thirst, screwed up menstrual periods and, most of all, cravings. I was only purging once every few weeks which was a significant improvement from every day. I also felt good about myself. I think mostly this was attributed to exercise, which I enjoyed. I felt stronger and more confident. On my graduation day I was able to fit in a very sleek mermaid-like gown and I actually for once in my life thought I looked beautiful.

My recovery never did materialize. In fact, things spiraled downward fast and furiously after graduation. That fall I moved to the big city to attend business college. I was on my own sharing an apartment with one of my best friends. I was excited and scared at the same time. I was away from my parents and had complete freedom for the first time in my life to decide what to do and not do.

I may have not been ready or mature enough for my new living arrangement but I certainly was going to take full advantage of it. I started partying a lot with new college friends and eating out every day. I was stressed from my new environment and at times felt overwhelmed. School was demanding with homework and missing classes would put you far behind. Of course, this is exactly what I did because I felt too fat to go. There were days I just didn't cope well and wanted to hide from the world. I started eating again to soothe my anxiety and comfort my feelings of insecurity. I was a small-town girl in a big city and my self-esteem again was hitting bottom.

Purging became part of my life again and was occurring daily if not twice a day. I had easy access to fast food and grocery stores only a few blocks away. With total control over what food I had in my apartment, my choices all focused on bingeing. Everything fell apart. I ended up quitting school and moved back home to my parents. Not only did I feel like a failure, but I felt bloated and fat from the twenty extra pounds I gained over the previous nine months of eating and drinking. It was the lowest point of my life and I hated how I looked.

Another path

My recovery didn't come fully until after I was married. My bingeing and purging episodes were declining after I had first moved in with my boyfriend. It was a very tiny apartment and secretly purging was not an easy feat. He was a fairly healthy person and didn't stray far from healthy foods. I started learning about eating healthier and had less and less interest in bingeing. The only time I would lose control is when I would go to my parents' house for supper or at special events when there was an abundance of food. I would sneak off and purge, telling myself it would be the last time. I wanted to quit so desperately because it had gone on for so long and I was exhausted from trying to hide my disgusting little secret.

I was finally able to stop when I found out I was pregnant. We had just gotten married and I was feeling nauseous a few weeks after. Ironically, I hated the feeling of having to throw up. When I learned I was pregnant I knew that it wasn't just about me anymore and that I had to ensure I ate well and kept food down. It was a very difficult time for me as my anxiety was unbearable when I overate. To me, the sensation of being full was a hundred times worse than feeling hungry. I was not used to seeing or feeling my stomach bloated and it was agonizing to fight the urge to purge. I would have to go for a long walk after big meals to keep myself away from the bathroom.

I kept telling myself that I would lose all my weight after the baby was born and that gaining weight was part of the pregnancy program. The cravings got worse than ever with hormones all over the place. I started eating sugary foods daily trying to fulfill my insatiable sweet cravings. But I was doing it; I was keeping everything down. And then, at the end of my pregnancy with only seven weeks left until my due date, I lost the baby. It was a blow I never saw coming. My body betrayed me again.

There was no explanation from the doctors and I was left feeling it was something I did wrong. What did I do? What did I do to my baby? These thoughts consumed me, along with hatred of my body betraying me again. I felt little support from my husband as he withdrew trying to deal with his own pain. I fell back into my bulimia to cope with my own grief. It was a pain I had never experienced before and it hurt so deeply I could hardly breathe. I self-medicated with food. Freshly baked chocolate cake and cookies were the drugs of choice.

Most of the time, I would bake just to eat the raw dough. My episodes lasted another year until we decided to try again for another baby. I knew I had to get healthy and I forced myself to keep everything down.

I had to do it like everyone else and face the consequences of overeating. If that meant I would be 20 pounds heavier, then so be it. I had a husband so who was I trying to starve myself for? Whose criticisms really did I care about? The only one harshly judging me was *me*.

This, I believe to this day, was my turning point. I finally gave myself the power to be who I am and to start loving myself. I had to erase the negative messages that I thought were guarding me against future hurts and disappointments. I had to take control over my thoughts about my weight and stop worrying about controlling food. My character and self-esteem were no longer going to be defined by a number on a scale. A year later I gave birth to a healthy baby boy.

Social worker and food advocate

Fast forward twenty years: Mother of two boys and a social worker, I was again at a pivotal turning point. I held a supervisory position which involved after-hours calls and intense workload pressures. My schedule after work usually involved picking up the boys from day care and throwing together a supper meal in fifteen minutes. My adrenaline was depleted by the time five o'clock came around and I had no brain cells left to be creative in regard to meal preparation. Knowing this was usually the case, I made sure I had semi-prepared meals that could be thrown in the oven or microwave. If I didn't have overly-processed foods available I would pick up fast food through the drive-thru on my way home which was at least twice a week. The best part about take-out was that there was no mess, which gave me more free time in the evening to relax.

My youngest son, Chase, was struggling in school. He was in Grade 3 and I had noticed he had been having trouble keeping up with his peers over the last couple years. At home he was disorganized, forgetful and scattered but because he was the "baby" I had always given him slack. He had constant anxiety about failing his grade and I always reassured him that he was not going to fail. Every night I went over his homework and tried to help him by playing fun learning games so he wouldn't get discouraged. I noticed his self-confidence plummeting and I didn't want to show him my own anxiety over his struggles.

His teachers were very supportive and had always made positive comments on his gentle and friendly demeanor. They said he would need extra support from the Resource Room. They also put in a referral for an educational psychological assessment. This came as a bit of a shock for me as I was usually involved in these types of assessments as a professional member of a counseling team and now my own son was going to be at the receiving end of one.

When the school Resource Room teacher phoned to discuss the results of the assessment she warned me that some of it may be tough to hear. My stomach hit the floor and a lump started to form in my throat. I had experience with this through my job and I knew that it was going to be a difficult road for him. I had seen it first hand through several clients and tried suppress the panic that was rising in my chest.

At the assessment meeting with the educational psychologist and my son's school team, the pattern they saw is that he couldn't concentrate on and retain information. He was scoring severely low in many areas, especially comprehension of material. His anxiety was pronounced when he was felt lost and he was aware he was falling behind.

I was told by the educational psychologist that he had all the symptoms of Attention Deficit Disorder and anxiety. I was handed a copy of the assessment and their recommendations for his teacher next year.

I started envisioning all the difficulties I saw former clients go through—the loss of self-esteem, skipping school or quitting school, turning to marijuana to deal with anxiety and resisting taking medication. As a social worker, I knew that all I had to do was pass this on to a psychiatrist and Chase would be prescribed medication. I wasn't going to go that road, yet. There had to be alternatives and I was desperate to seek them out.

Food and the brain

I remembered reading articles on how some foods affect moods and behavior. I figured it was a good place to start. I had purchased some books on topics about foods and the brain. I also commenced a furious Internet investigation on how to manage symptoms of ADD and anxiety. I found an amazing abundance of information that has actually been available for the past twenty years. I wondered, why has this not been brought to the attention of the general public? There has been a vast amount of ongoing research on the brain's abilities that most of us don't know about. In the past five years, new, exciting research was showing that we have the ability to change our brains. This was great news. One of the methods described was through a healthy diet. I learned that foods had a direct affect on the brain and there were foods that would reduce the efficiency of the brain and foods that would enhance it. Bingo! I had somewhere to start.

I was on a mission and the first thing I learned was that everything I had been feeding my children since their birth had been bad brain food. Not only bad for their brain, but bad for their development in general. How was I to know this? As a mother I was in charge of meeting their nutritional needs but wasn't given any lessons or instructions. Most of what I learned was through television ads, marketing, or my own mother. The majority of my grocery choices were about convenience, and not having to fight with my kids to eat their food. So macaroni and cheese with hot dogs was a staple in my house. It was quick and they loved it.

If I was going to help my son, I had to change everything about our eating. This meant meal planning, cooking and (most of all) weaning ourselves away from poor, unhealthy foods that we not only loved, but we were in fact addicted to. That included my own addictions such as my 3 p.m. Diet Coke, the sweeteners in my coffee and my precious gummy candies that I relied on for a pick-me-up. I knew there were many challenges I would be dealing with, but giving up wasn't an option.

Within two years of revamping our entire diet and eliminating processed foods, my son made the honor roll. He was starting to enjoy school and his confidence was beaming from every pore. He went from the shy, nervous student who wished he was invisible to a kid full of wit and an infectious spirit for life. It was as though another brain was plunked in his skull. I was happy that his kindness and compassion for others remained.

The moral of the story

This may sound like a success story, but it wasn't easy. Initially I had resistance from everyone in my family, and there were times when my children refused to eat their supper. I knew they wouldn't starve and that they would eventually eat the fruit and vegetables that were put out and available. My husband loved his take out and fast food. He was the last to follow the "program." He was an adult and had to make his own choices. I couldn't force him to do anything and my ranting wasn't helping either. I suppose his older brother's unexpected death from his first heart attack made him start thinking about prevention. It validates my social work mantra that we seem to suddenly decide to make changes when a crisis falls upon us.

Today I am a different person, inside and out. I have never felt so amazing in my life. I am more resilient to stress and to the latest cold and flu bug going around. My youthful energy is coming back, my confidence is soaring and my skin is glowing. It was a difficult transition from eating badly to eating well, but worth every struggle. Although I had recovered from bulimia, I was still a food addict and using food to deal with my overwhelming life and work pressures.

My family and I went from eating fast food twice a week to once a year (sometimes not even). White sugar is no longer in the house, which is what I mostly lived on most of my adolescent years and was my "crack" as an adult. There is little food in my cupboard that comes in a box and cooking no longer seems to be a chore. I used to obsess about calories, fat and weight gain but now my goal is well-being and disease prevention. I still love food but my choices are much different. I now eat to live and no longer live to eat.

I came from the pit of hell in regard to compulsive eating and can honestly say I am a recovered emotional eater. My goal is to help others understand that we are brainwashed to control calories and we judge ourselves when we can't limit them. How we view ourselves and food *increases* our chances of having an unhealthy relationship with food.

To make it tougher, the landscape of food around us is addicting and the pressures of life are overwhelming. The food industry and our culture also work against us. With so many factors involved in our convoluted relationship with food, it's no wonder so many people are struggling. Foods can help us and foods can harm us.

Food used to be my coping mechanism, therefore food kept me hostage for a very long time. It kept me in its strong clasp disguising itself as relief from guilt, anxiety, hopeless-ness and disempowerment. Food meets our emotional needs but only temporarily, leaving us in more anguish. We need to start repairing our emotional foundation by digging deep and facing our demons. Food dependency is a progression; not always an event. Is there a pain or emotional discomfort you are avoiding? Is your self-esteem bottomed out? There is a correlation between mood and food and we need to identify what emotional needs we are addressing with food.

My hope is that my story and this little book will shake your common thinking about food and dieting. I acknowledge I am not a doctor, or a dietician, and yet, I am writing a book about food and emotion. I may even be challenged for doing so. But I am an expert on my own experience with emotional eating, and with what I have learned on my personal journey. I am an expert on what worked and didn't work for me.

As a social worker, I have a professional awareness of the underlying reasons for our behavior and that our environment molds our self-esteem and influences our world-view.

As a passionate advocate for my clients, those in audiences I speak to and do workshops with and those reading this book, I want to share what I have learned, and hopefully provide hope to others who feel trapped in the prison of emotional eating.

As a mother, I wanted the best for my children and their future and I had to acquire a new set of skills and tools that were initially unfamiliar to me in order to do that. I want to empower other parents who are already overwhelmed with responsibilities that eating better is not really that difficult and reaps many benefits.

We may share some similarities, and undoubtedly have many differences. But I have been where you are. I can assure you that I did not think I would overcome these challenges. I did, however, and I believe you can too. I hope my anguish gives you solace and my story rallies you to triumph over your own emotional eating.

CHAPTER 1

MIND + EMOTIONS = BEHAVIORS

"Sow an action and you reap a habit. Sow
a habit and you reap a character. Sow a
character and you reap a destiny."

Quintilian

Reprogram your ideas about food

We live in a culture that is trying to bulk us up. Temptation is lurking around every corner and we feel we need to pick and choose when we are going to let ourselves be pulled in. How many conversations have you had with yourself such as, "Oh, I shouldn't today" or "Well, I haven't treated myself for a while"? Using food as a reward becomes a positive reinforcement for emotional eating. We have the belief that food is a desired reward, therefore we pursue food increasing its power in the urge-pursuit-reward cycle or habit. How many times have you heard a mother say to her child, "If you aren't good you will not get a treat"? This food-is-a-reward mentality starts at a very young age and becomes stronger in our adult lives.

We also have traditions and values associated with foods, especially desserts. Birthdays, Christmas and family gatherings usually have an abundance of appealing desserts and treats that are hard to resist. The showing of love and affection is also accompanied by preparing or baking special sugary treats for those we care about. Strong connections between food and memories are ingrained in our brains because of the positive emotional response that experience provided to us. This memory-emotional food process results in "treating ourselves" with sugary treats or starchy junk foods. We rationalize our caving in to our cravings as something we deserve because we worked so hard or we were "good" yesterday.

We need to start reprogramming our ideas about food in order for permanent good eating habits to form. Our bodies are designed to ingest natural food. Long before grocery stores, restaurants and vending machines came along, nature provided all that was needed in order for our bodies and minds to heal, balance and function effectively. Food was so effective in providing the nutrients our bodies needed that the traditional medicine passed on from one generation to another utilized natural plants, herbs, and roots in its healing methods. For every ailment or wound there was a natural healing solution.

Today we have a tendency to put all our trust in manufactured solutions that are created with synthetic processes. This includes foods with flavors and additives derived from chemicals that are used to attract consumers with a strong appeal. "The food industry is not only generating billions of dollars for itself by designing hyperpalatable combinations of sugar, fat and salt—it's also creating products that have the capability to rewire brains, driving us to seek out more and more of those products." *(The End of Overeating, David A. Kessler, MD, 2009)* Natural foods are "enhanced" by flavors and chemicals turning food into something else. Most of the natural ingredients are manipulated or stripped from their original state resulting in food that our bodies are not biologically adapted to digest. Could these newly designed foods pose some risk to our overall health? With obesity, Type 2 Diabetes and depression rates soaring, one would have difficulty arguing that they don't.

"Over the past one hundred years our cancer mortality rate has gone from 3 percent of all deaths to 20 percent of all deaths. Our incidence of diabetes went from 0.1 percent of the population to almost 20 percent. Heart disease went from being almost nonexistent to killing more than seven hundred thousand people per year. At the same time, health care costs have risen until the United States now spends twice as much on medicine and care per person per year than any other industrialized nation in the world." *(The Hundred Year Lie, Randall Fitzgerald, 2006)* We may think our world is progressing, however our foods are deteriorating in their ability to efficiently provide us with the nutrients we need physically and psychologically.

Foods can heal and foods can hurt. We have a tendency to gravitate towards refined, processed foods in order to feel short-term pleasure. If we truly want to reward or treat ourselves or loved ones, we need to choose foods that will make us feel good for a longer period. We deserve to be healthy, we deserve to be disease-free and we deserve to have our bodies and minds nourished to live a long and happy life. Create new positive eating patterns by forming a lasting desire to want better natural health for yourself.

"If we aren't willing to settle for junk living, we certainly shouldn't settle for junk food."

Sally Edward

Our battle with food obsession

Although we may not readily admit it, we all obsess about something. It could be our jobs, our children, sports, shoes, or an annoying behavior of a partner or coworker. Unfortunately, the preoccupation with food and body image seems to be hitting an all time high in North America. There probably isn't a day that goes by when you haven't seen an advertisement or front-page article on "How to Lose Weight

Quickly" or an image of the "ideal" body type. But remember for every new diet ad there is a clever captive-marketing ploy from the fast food industry profoundly influencing your appetite. The enticements of junk-food or fast food ads are lurking around every corner inviting us into that first bite, stimulating our senses to want more. Children are the most vulnerable as most advertising strategies are geared towards them, putting them at risk of childhood obesity.

This tug of war between dieting and our appetite for junk foods is creating a food obsession. Food obsessions are characterized by food and weight. Obsession with food creates constant thinking about food, eating and then bingeing resulting in weight-gain. As the fear or dread of weight-gain kicks in, we condemn ourselves to stop eating. Our efforts to control our eating will more likely fail miserably because we tend to take the all-or-nothing approach. Most dieters highly restrict their food or calorie intake, which usually is nutritionally deficient or boring. This way of eating is difficult to sustain and will precipitate bingeing, making us feel like failures. When we're feeling low and repeating negative messages to ourselves it will trigger a need for comfort and that soothing relief we know comes from food. In the end, dieting puts our emotional health and self-esteem in the dumps.

Obesity rates are climbing even though the diet industry is making profits in the billions. Education about nutrition and exercise is not enough to fight obesity. Our environment, culture and economic status play significant roles and the increase in obesity rates is becoming a natural result of our way of life. If you do not want to become a victim of the fast food culture, the first place to start is to wean yourself from junk-food thinking. Start thinking about getting rid of something harmful rather than something you value.

**Here are some practices to move away from
food and weight obsession:**

- Limit TV watching or walk away from commercials.

- Read more information on topics that speak about holistic
  health and not primarily weight-loss.

- Focus on shopping the perimeter of the grocery store, not
  the inside aisles. Fresh foods are on the perimeter and most
  processed foods are shelved in middle aisles.

- Read food labels for nutritional value, not calories. Powerful
  appeal comes through cleverly designed packaging and "Low
  Calorie" or "Low Fat" bold lettering. Look for foods high in fiber.

- If eating out, choose a relaxing, sit-down atmosphere to enjoy fresh,
  high quality food. Focus on the conversation and surroundings.

- Acknowledge that the messages our culture gives us daily may
  not be in our best interest. Go against the grain even though
  not everyone is going to agree or join your new lifestyle.

- Thinking of eating healthy as a long commitment and not just a
  six-week plan.

- Absorb your own messages by putting up written signs by your
  work-station or kitchen such as, "If it doesn't nourish my body and
  mind, it's junk. I DESERVE better!"

- Nothing eases shame more than finding support and sharing. Empower yourself by reaching out for counselling, or find support from others who are working towards obtaining a healthier lifestyle.

We mistakenly put most of the blame on ourselves for over-eating when our culture and media constantly promote it. We need to acknowledge there are a lot of mixed messages around us and we need to start exploring our own truths. Start obsessing and researching about health (physical, emotional, mental and spiritual) and not body image and you will look better, feel better and live better.

You're not that different from your dog

If you have ever taken a psychology class, whether in high school or college, you have likely heard of Ivan Pavlov and his experiment on dogs, dubbed "Pavlov's Dogs." In the 19th century, Pavlov studied the natural behavioral response of dogs when they would see food. When food would come in the direction of the dogs they would salivate. This was considered an in-born natural behavior.

When Pavlov introduced the ringing of a bell, just before the food would come, there was no response. However, when this procedure was repeated over and over, the dogs started salivating every time they heard the bell ring. The dogs recognized the bell as a cue for food, which generated a response from their saliva glands. Pavlov realized through his experiment that behaviors can be conditioned or instilled. We are not that different from dogs, as human behavior is shaped by past experiences.

To take this experiment one step further, my husband takes our dog with him on Saturdays to run his errands. His first stop is always the drive-thru to pick up a morning coffee. The regular place he goes always offers a small deep-fried, sugar-coated "donut hole" to our dog. After a few months of this our dog can now recognize the branding of this coffee-donut chain. She salivates when it is in sight and practically jumps through the window when he drives into the parking lot. Of course this was an accidental discovery, but it certainly demonstrates the power of food and memory.

The behavioral conditioning that can be applied to dogs surely can be applied to humans. Knowing that fat, sugar and salt (especially all combined) are extremely addicting, imagine if we connect enjoying them to a repeated activity, place or emotion. How many of us associate watching a movie with eating junk foods or boredom with snacking?

Evenings, when we watch TV, are one of the most common times we snack and this is no secret to the food industry. Fast food, pizza and junk-food companies advertise heavily in the evenings reminding you that their food is the missing element to your TV-watching. Therefore, the best thing you can do is walk away during commercials to protect yourself from this stimulus.

The good news is that we can recondition ourselves but it takes repetition, repetition, and repetition. Eventually these new behaviors will become automatic. Although we may never fully lose our old behaviors, our awareness of what may trigger unwanted responses is an important skill to have. Being mindful of your environment, your routine and your feelings is the first step to recognizing whether you are conditioned.

List 3 activities that you associate with food:

1. _____
2. _____
3. _____

List 3 emotions that lead you towards unhealthy foods:

1. _____
2. _____
3. _____

How are these associations with foods harmful to your emotional, mental and physical health?

_____

_____

_____

_____

_____

_____

_____

_____

Emotions, thoughts and actions

Human beings are the most privileged species on Earth. Our minds are not only more advanced but we are able to feel. Humans are emotional beings. This may make some men or even women cringe as some presume that emotions make us weak, irrational, or even out of control. But all humans have emotions and they are a very important part of who we are as people. They make us unique and exciting.

Emotions are part of our human experience. They help us connect with one another and become a social society. They also contribute to deeper learning, such as when we have a strong emotion around a certain experience we will never forget, and that memory will help us make decisions in the future. Our subconscious stores these memories, good or bad, and calls upon them when a similar situation stands before us again. Emotions play a significant role in how we respond to experiences and to one another.

Negative thoughts have a tendency to distort our feelings. There's a strong relationship between thoughts and feelings as thoughts drive our feelings. Negative thoughts drain our emotional energy and motivation causing dissatisfaction in our lives. An example would be unnecessarily worrying all night about a situation causing you to be exhausted the next day. The excessive worrying results in feeling crummy and tired, putting you at risk of making poor choices.

There are also negative and positive emotions. Most of us would prefer to experience only positive emotions as they give us feelings of pleasure, satisfaction, joy, comfort, and self-confidence. However, negative emotions have their place as they create change, growth, progress and even self-confidence. The trick is in managing these emotions and finding the lessons behind them. By accepting your anger, sadness, and embarrassment as part of yourself, you will move closer to an understanding of your true self.

Our behaviors are a direct result of our thoughts and feelings and if we want to change our behavior we first need to change our way of thinking. We need to move from our regular thought patterns in order to develop new possibilities. To accomplish new feelings and behaviors it's important to know what messages your subconscious is holding. If they're not beneficial to your new goals, then you need to work hard at replacing them with practical and constructive ones.

Positive thinking is widely recognized and popular today as it is the key to a positive and fulfilling life. Positive thinking promotes positive feelings that provide high energy and a bright outlook. Fuelling good moods with ongoing positive thoughts encourages us to act the way we feel. Our actions and behaviors will bring forth our circumstances. As in *The Secret* by Rhonda Byrne, the saying, "thoughts become things," rings true. We can realize many things in our lives through our thinking. The objective is to manage our emotions by purging unproductive thoughts and replacing them with intentional positive thoughts to open the way to a more rewarding life.

You are what you think

Whether we are pursuing a dream or establishing a goal we need to learn how to be our own best cheerleaders. Far too often we beat ourselves down with constant negative self-chatter. So many of the negative criticisms we say to ourselves end up buried in our subconscious minds ready to pop out whenever we have an obstacle in front of us. Our subconscious, containing mostly toxic negative messages, robs us of our will and well-being. How many times a week have you criticized yourself or discouraged yourself from trying something new? This negative thinking deflates our self-esteem and confidence dampening our dreams and hopes. How has your self-criticism helped you? How many times has beating yourself down assisted you in accomplishing a goal? It doesn't. In fact, it only keeps you down, making you expect and accept failure and disappointment. It is time to get rid of these false beliefs and expect more for yourself.

Positive thinking helps in many ways. Believing that your goals are attainable is the first step as it gives you the courage to try. Having helpful and supportive thoughts nurtures patience if you happen to stumble. Positive thinking also helps you manage when surprises occur and prevents you from falling into past emotional booby traps. Pat yourself on the back, even for accomplishing minor tasks, and you will start to boost your morale. Positive thinking induces positive feelings which give us happiness, peace, and joy.

Our subconscious is built from past emotions, memories and experiences and it can be rebuilt. Choose to reject negative thoughts and replace them with positive thoughts. Don't dismiss the power of your thoughts; be wary of accepting self-demoralizing messages. Start by reframing messages about yourself and celebrating little successes no matter how small. Compliment yourself. Go ahead; even feel self-righteous about it! You probably could use some self-inflating thoughts so don't worry about sounding conceited. Fill your mind with concepts of happiness, success, and self-love.

Replacing your negative thoughts with positive ones will increase your optimism and bring you energy. If you have difficulty shutting down the negative messages whirling around in your head, write down positive messages to yourself every day and state them out loud over and over.

Your brain will absorb these messages and lock them in your subconscious providing fuel for your next goal.

Repetition of positive messages will unleash an internal power and impact everything around you. Envision who you want to be and don't be afraid of possible pitfalls. Remember: what you say about yourself in the inside will manifest on the outside. You are what you think, so stop living inside negative thoughts and start living out loud by being your own cheerleader.

Targeting self-defeating behaviors

If you want to make a significant change in your life you need to make adjustments to your attitude and behavior. Many people desire the end results but do not want to commit to the steps required to get there or feel they will fail halfway through. If you haven't made up your mind about doing things differently then it will end there, "after all, before people will change their behaviors, they have to want to do so, and this means that they'll have to think differently." *(The Influencer, The Power to Change Anything, 2008)*

If you have decided you are ready to make some changes, because doing the same thing over and over is no longer working for you, then you are in position to take the first step. And the first step is to identify those behaviors that are not helping you reach your goals. It is very difficult to confront our behaviors as we tend to become quite comfortable with our own excuses. Trying to influence someone to change can be difficult; changing your own behavior is no easier.

When it comes to identifying problematic eating behaviors, the easiest way to become aware of them is to observe how you cope or recover from an emotionally charged event or day. Do you tend to gravitate towards certain foods? What is the first solution that comes to you when stressed? It is helpful to log a week of events and foods consumed to see if there is a link. This may require some effort, but it is essential to recognize where improvements are needed.

We need to replace our current self-defeating behaviors with more positive ones. To begin, identify behaviors that are interfering with your goals. Then determine some good replacements—actions that will support rather than defeat those goals. For example, if you and your supervisor have a heated disagreement, which is leading you to the vending machine afterwards, you need to have a better solution ready in your head. What is a better solution in this situation? You can go for a quick, five-minute walk to burn off some energy and frustration or ask a co-worker for support through this difficult time. If you still crave that snack, allow yourself time to make some healthier choices. In order for replacement behaviors to be effective you need to plan ahead. As many habits are ingrained, it's going to take some mental effort to follow through on your new improved choices. The inevitable bad day will come and you need to be prepared for it. Having healthy snacks stashed somewhere (or everywhere) that are quickly accessible or keeping a pair of comfortable walking shoes in your car or by your desk will prevent you from falling back on old habits.

Another common behavior is deflecting blame or responsibility. There are countless people who really would like to lose weight but say they can't because of their spouses, children, jobs, or stressful events like a divorce. There are times when these excuses don't even make sense. Does the blame of polishing off a whole pan of puffed wheat cake fall on the shoulders of your children?

Taking responsibility for your eating behaviors is essential in order to come to the understanding that you are in charge of what goes in your mouth. There are times when you are faced with limited choices, but you can still limit the amount you eat. Many people rationalize bad choices as there is so much guilt, denial and shame around the topic of weight-loss. Denial is a stuck state of mind; acceptance is the opposite. By accepting your behavior you are moving forward and that's progress.

Trying new behaviors is not going to come naturally. It is going to take keen awareness of your feelings and lots of practice. New is good but not always easy. "Think of old habits as built-up scar-tissue, thick, inflexible and rigid—which limits your range of motion. Your job is to slowly, carefully and deliberately break those bonds, so that you can create new, more fluid and desirable connections." *(Retraining Your Brain, Dr. Frank Lawlis, 2009)* There are times when you are going to slip into what is comfortable, sometimes without even thinking about it. Take advantage of these situations as learning experiences, recover from them and move on. Once you start mastering a new behavior, your self-esteem will be boosted and your determination enhanced. Don't underestimate the little changes in self-improvement—sometimes results will reveal themselves when you aren't even looking.

Is your guilt really motivating you?

Whether it is about eating healthier, joining a running class, getting a project completed or spending more time with loved ones we from time to time struggle to meet our goals. Guilt then pops its ugly head and shakes its finger at us expressing its disappointment in our actions (or lack of) making us hang our head in shame.

Guilt is actually a response from our subconscious which can be an important tool to life lessons, and keep us following a code of behaviors, maintaining important relationships and keeping us out of jail! It's also good in regards to the human race feeling a sense of responsibility to each other and the world. But if your guilt has nothing to do with doing something illegal and immoral then it can become a self-inflicted and prosecuting emotion that causes anxiety, worry, on-going grief and low self-worth. Guilt can be very unhealthy and paralyzing.

Guilt played a very significant role in my eating disorder and was always by my side. It never stopped talking and always kept reminding me of what I should have and shouldn't have done. Guilt made me eat so I could dull its constant chattering; guilt made me purge and then belittled me afterward. Guilt defined me. It took a long time for me to recognize its power and how it was sucking the life out of me.

If we start exploring guilt at a deeper level, we can see that it usually is combined with other feelings such as shame, unworthiness, remorse, regret, dissatisfaction, and helplessness. Guilt can put you in a victimized state even when it is self-inflicted. It can linger and take root never allowing you to feel peace. To start addressing your guilt, you must start questioning and challenging your guilt. Ask yourself, "Is my guilt rational?" "What do I hope to accomplish by feeling guilty?' "Is my guilt productive?" "Is my guilt burdening me or anyone else around me?" "What would relieve my guilt?" When you feel guilt rising in your chest and anxiety filling your lungs, take a deep breath and face it.

Guilt should not play the lead role in motivating you toward your goals, especially weight-loss goals. Guilt does not serve your best interests and can prevent you from moving forward. If you have a gym membership that you haven't used for a year and you keep paying on it, you need to cancel it. Stop torturing yourself and wasting your money. Accept and move on to find other means of physical activity that you may enjoy. Guilty feelings can stem from failure so stop continually setting yourself up. Make a small realistic goal preventing you from feeling overwhelmed. We can't do it all and we have stop continuing to think so.

Life is about growth and change and not always about what we define as right and wrong. We sometimes take two steps forward and one step back but we are still moving forward. Our intentions don't always work out but we have the opportunity to learn from the situation and forgive ourselves. Relieve yourself from this emotional toxin. Do this through self-forgiveness, planning for success and acknowledging all that you do.

Change is going to be uncomfortable

Whether you are thinking about quitting smoking, getting a new job, or trying a new hairstyle you may feel nervous about stepping out of your comfort zone. Change can bring anxiety even if you are excited about the end results. We are creatures of habit and are comfortable with routines and what we know. However, whatever is not working for you right now needs to be changed. The old saying, "You are not going to get a different result by doing the same thing over and over" holds true. Making a slight shift in an action or decision will bring a new result. This includes weight loss and health goals.

Many of us have tried different weight loss strategies throughout our lives. Some people have been successful but many have not. The weight loss industry actually knows that most people will be back trying and trying again. A person like this is called a repeat customer. Most diet regimes cannot be maintained long term, never mind for the rest of our lives. As human beings we hate having our rights restricted, especially when eating is a basic need. Weight loss diets in the last 20 years have usually consisted of low-fat or low-carb menus, giving us the impression that carbs and fats are bad. Our bodies need carbohydrates and good fats and some of them are, in fact, essential for good physical and mental health. This old-school way of thinking is going to be uncomfortable to change.

Carbohydrates and good fats

Carbohydrates are split into two categories: simple carbohydrates and complex carbohydrates. Simple carbs are those that we reach for when we need a quick pick-me-up. These foods are usually processed, refined and filled with sugar or sweeteners. These include white flour and white rice products such as white bread and rice cakes. They usually have no nutritional value, cause sugar levels to spike quickly and induce inflammation in the body.

Simple carbs bring a fast surge of relief but the soon-to-come sugar crash will have us in a worse physical and mental state than before. These carbs make up a large percentage of many people's diets as refined, processed carbs are addicting, convenient and accessible. Eliminating these carbs is going to be uncomfortable as they give us temporary pleasure and relief from our daily pressures.

Complex carbohydrates such as whole grains, whole-grain cereals and breads, whole-wheat pastas, vegetables and fruits contain fiber which keeps sugar levels more stable and which meets many nutritional needs for the body. Vegetables, especially green leafy vegetables, are the top choice as they have premium nutrients that help repair and restore cells. The most valuable property of carbohydrates is that they help produce brain chemicals that make us feel good. When our blood sugar starts to take a dip, we feel cranky, tired and hungry. Complex carbohydrates raise blood sugar at a slower and steadier pace and they help replenish the mood-boosting chemical, serotonin. Being choosy about carbohydrates can bring beneficial and long-lasting results.

Fat is the most misunderstood macronutrient. Most diets focus on minimizing fat consumption. However, you cannot lose weight without eating fat. Restricting fat intake will alert the hormone, leptin, that there is a decrease of fat in the bloodstream. Leptin makes the brain aware of the lower levels and messages are sent for you to eat more fat. Eating good fats will keep fat levels in the blood stable; therefore leptin will remain at ease, which is helpful in reducing cravings.

Some sources of good fats are:
- Almonds, cashews, walnuts
- Pumpkin and sunflower seeds
- Olive oil, grape seed oil
- Avocado, guacamole
- Nut butters
- Coconut oil
- Flaxseed, flax oil
- Fish oils

Many people see these items filled with fat and calories and avoid them at all costs. This is where a new way of thinking may be uncomfortable. However, fat has many important roles including keeping our skin and other organs healthy. "Fat-free diets are a one-way ticket to trouble. Fat and oils provide anti-inflammatory and antioxidant protections" *(The Perricone Prescription, Nicholas Perricone, M.D.)* Good fats are becoming recognized for strengthening the immune system and reducing inflammation. The most appealing thing about eating good fats is that they aid in weight loss and give us a feeling of satisfaction after consumption. Realizing that fat is your friend is going to take some getting used to. But then again, change is good.

Are you an emotional eater?

Westerners are eating the most stressed-out diet on the planet. The foods we choose to soothe our fears, comfort our anxieties and relax our tensions actually exacerbate the stress we are feeling. After an emotionally taxing day we tend to reach for sugar or refined carbs to improve our moods. With our hormones continually adapting to all the events we encounter or the tasks demanded of us, the hormonal imbalance at the end of the day will lead us to that package of cookies in our cupboard as soon as we walk in the door. "The psychological experience is as much involved as the biological experience." *(Why Women Need Chocolate, Debra Waterhouse, MPH, RD, 1995)*

Sugar boosts the good-mood hormone, serotonin. Serotonin provides us with the feeling of joy, satisfaction and confidence. When our serotonin levels are low, our brain does what it can to bring them back to normal by sending out messages that we call cravings. The combination of fat and sugar is most desirable to women as fat lifts our endorphin levels. Endorphin is a pain-relieving hormone that is as powerful as morphine. Most women report that cravings are more intense during their menstrual cycle. We are unable to resist the strong messages from the brain as it tries to keep hormones at their appropriate levels. Therefore, as good-mood hormones dip, we are left with uncontrollable sugar and fat cravings that are nearly impossible to resist.

The key to ensuring proper good-mood hormone levels is to eat foods that maintain stable blood sugar levels. If the brain is supplied with maximum energy throughout the day, from "healthy" carbohydrates, proteins and good fats, it will provide us with alertness, creative thinking and stable moods. Our resiliency, when life demands it, depends on eating healthy meals that will sustain us. If our blood sugar levels drop and we "starve" the brain, it will protest with headaches, irritability and fatigue. When low energy and unclear thinking occur, we lose our self-control and rationale around food, putting us at risk of making some very poor choices to fulfill these very immediate and urgent needs.

Three top mood saboteurs, that we continually use to lift our moods and restore our energy, are sugar, sugar substitutes, and refined starches. All are usually found in refined, processed snacks or sugary, store-bought treats such as cookies, cakes, doughnuts, muffins, crackers, cereals, and sweetened drinks and colas. As they provide little nutritional value and contain additives that are addicting, they are not only toxic to our bodies but also to our moods.

Here is how this process works: Within a minute of consuming a diet cola and cookie your body becomes highly stressed trying to neutralize the destructive impact of these "foods." First your body sends out adrenaline, the "fight or flight" hormone, as it senses your body is being attacked. Then endorphin and serotonin levels go up, making you feel good temporarily. Insulin is called onto the scene to deal with the excessively high blood sugar and it also tells your body to store fat. After insulin has completed its job your energy and mental stamina start to plummet, which brings forward your stress hormone, cortisol, to release emergency sugar stores from the liver so you don't pass out. As cortisol doesn't usually feel pleasant it motivates us to get rid of it by, you guessed it, reaching for a sugary snack again. This process can happen two to four times a day putting great strain on our hormones, affecting our moods and increasing our chances of weight gain.

This vicious emotional eating cycle can rapidly form into a dependency when our feelings are intense and sugary food relieves us. Also, the more frequently we use bad foods to fix our bad moods the more entrenched the behavior becomes. In order for an intervention to happen we need to recognize how our habits are contributing to the stress-eating cycle. It seems the worse we feel, the worse we are at taking care of ourselves. There are a variety of healthier choices that will provide our bodies and minds with the essential nutrients needed to function optimally. We can eliminate emotional eating from taking over our lives and have the quality of life we are seeking just by nourishing our brains and bodies with the right foods.

Emotional eating

For people living under emotional distress, every day forces them to seek out a positive surge of relief. This relief can feel satisfactory even for five or ten minutes of the day. Food becomes the major source of this comfort. Turning to comfort food is a learned behavior as we realize that food makes us feel better, motivating us to repeat the behavior without much thought. Indulging in these foods was initially started by the strong positive emotional response from what we ate and this resulted in the regular craving for this food. Eventually this behavior becomes firmly established and develops into a very hard habit to break. Almost like an addiction!

Sugar and carbohydrates can be powerful tranquilizers for many people. Food soothes, calms, and alleviates anxiety. The pleasure from food arouses such emotions as satisfaction, happiness, and delight. It becomes wired in our brains that foods are rewarding and should be sought after when we are feeling crummy. Eventually food becomes a coping mechanism for those living under extreme stress or emotional turmoil. The long-term effects of using food to cope with life, especially sugary or fat-loaded foods, are obesity, health-related problems and depression.

The good news is that there are many healthy, emotionally soothing or mood-enhancing foods. There are foods armed with nutrients and essential amino acids that can provide elevated moods and satisfaction. Carbohydrates provide the necessary relief we are seeking.

Carbohydrates include whole-grain breads, whole-wheat pasta, brown or wild rice, barley, potatoes and sweet potatoes. Vegetables are also part of the carbohydrate family and are filled with most of the vital nutrients our bodies require for optimal functioning. The key is to have these foods available when we are feeling vulnerable.

Many people choose a low-carb, low-fat diet in order to lose weight fast. Going on a high protein diet with no carbohydrates will only bring short-term results as it is difficult if not impossible to sustain this type of diet long term. Dieting promotes emotional binge eating as it restricts certain foods that are helpful in making good-mood chemicals. Research has shown that carbohydrates assist in the making of the hormone serotonin. Julia Ross, author of *The Mood Cure* and *The Diet Cure* encourages her readers to choose fruits and vegetables instead of cookies and cake to boost serotonin levels.

Serotonin is one of the keys to controlling your appetite and minimizing the cravings for sugar and starches. Restricting carbohydrates will quickly deplete serotonin levels, making you feel drained and unsatisfied. The brain will start giving out strong signals to consume carbohydrates, which will result in cravings for these foods. It will be difficult to resist the signals as you will never feel satisfied or full from other non-carb foods. As a result, you may end up bingeing on unhealthy carbohydrates such as salty snacks, desserts or breads. This will bring some relief, however the lasting effects may show up on the bathroom scale.

The trick is to eat the right carbohydrates at the right time every day to curb cravings and avoid carb-bingeing. The majority of people crave carbohydrates pre-evening and throughout the night. To prevent carb-overloading after supper, have a half piece of whole grain bread dipped in olive oil twenty minutes before supper. This will raise your serotonin levels enough to take the edge off and prevent you from overeating at supper. During supper it is important to eat carbohydrates such as brown rice, sweet potatoes, or whole-wheat pasta. Be conscious of your portion sizes. In the evening, if cravings persist, try eating air-popped popcorn with a little butter and a hot cup of chamomile tea. Cravings can also be managed through stress-relieving strategies such as having a warm bath or reading a book in a quiet room. Sometimes it just requires us to step out of our hurried state, slow down, and breathe.

We may struggle at first as we tend to make choices that require less thought and energy. Breaking the emotional eating cycle demands our attention and persistence. Rewiring the brain and learning new behaviors takes time, patience, and planning. After some time we will find gratification from other healthier sources that de-stress us or give us pleasure, releasing us from the grasp of the emotional eating cycle.

Why are we feeling so crappy and cranky?

Our lifestyles have changed drastically from the time of our grandparents. We are no longer plowing the fields and tending to gardens to put food on the table for our families. We have many comforts and conveniences that only require the tip of our fingers. All we need to do to stay warm or remain cool is to turn a dial. Commuting to places no longer involves walking and owning a vehicle can provide a higher standard of living. Living in a developed country gives us a higher quality of life and opportunities galore. If this is the case, then why are we feeling so crummy?

Lack of sunlight / Lack of vitamin D

Being indoors under unnatural, bright lighting messes up our serotonin and melatonin levels, which we need for regulated sleep patterns. Vitamin D is also considered the miracle mood enhancer giving us the feeling of happiness. Today, most people are working eight hours or more indoors under fluorescent lighting and getting outdoors when the sun is going down. When we get fresh air and sunlight we immediately perk up!

Lack of sleep

Sleep rejuvenates the brain and body by repairing and replacing damaged and dying cells. It is like recharging a dying battery. Prior to 1930 people were getting nine hours of sleep. Today we are getting an average of seven to seven and a half hours of sleep falling into a huge sleep deficit. This is hard on the heart and brain and can result in cardiovascular diseases, poor memory recall and concentration. A good sleep keeps our sugar levels stable and appetite and cravings down. Also, during sleep, serotonin, is replenished in order to keep levels adequate and make us feel good.

Lack of exercise

There is no substitute for exercise; we need it to increase serotonin and dopamine levels. Sweating also excretes toxins from the body. Another benefit to exercise, besides toning and building muscle, is that it keeps our sugar/glucose levels stable resulting in less insulin being produced. The less we exercise the less we feel like exercising and the more we exercise the more we want to exercise. Exercise increases our energy levels. It goes beyond losing weight and looking great and takes only ten to fifteen minutes a day to feel the benefits.

Boring job/classes

Going to the same mediocre job or uninteresting classes reduces dopamine levels. Putting the brain on "autopilot" or "sleep mode" reduces mental activity until certain areas of the brain fizzle out. A happy brain is a working brain. If your day job is boring, find an activity or hobby that is going to require creativity, concentration and some happy time!

Modern food (Standard American Diet otherwise known as SAD)

Modern food processing has completely altered the types of fatty acids we consume, depriving us of what we need for normal brain development and repair. Most nutrients are destroyed during the processing of packaged foods, making meals less nutritious and depriving your body and brain of the fuel to function efficiently. Today we are overweight, but malnourished.

High sugar and insulin levels

Lots of sugar and carbohydrates lead to increased insulin levels. High insulin tells the body to store what you just ate as fat, dropping your blood sugar concentration. Your brain needs a consistent flow of glucose from food. Choosing foods that have natural sugars keeps the flow of glucose more regulated than sugary treats. Today we are experiencing high and low sugar spikes resulting in imbalanced insulin and serotonin levels creating low moods, depression and diabetes.

Deficiency in just one of these hormones will make you feel draggy and sluggish. Improper levels of two or more will result in your body and mind falling completely out of balance, making you tired, stressed, forgetful, depressed, irritable, unfocused and overweight.

Conquering emotional eating

Fad diets, with all their great intentions and methods to motivate us to eat healthier, don't address behavioral or emotional issues when it comes to eating. Emotions and moods are very powerful and can entice us into an emotional eating cycle without our even being aware of it. Emotional eating is a response to an incident, situation or feeling that is usually unpleasant or stressful. This usually causes a shift in our hormones or mood sending strong signals to seek out comfort foods. Our drive to emotional eating is linked to the demands and pressures we feel throughout the day. The first step in eliminating emotional eating is becoming aware of what foods we crave when we encounter certain situations or specific feelings. We typically associate foods with certain emotions.

Here are a few reasons we seek food to perk us up:
- Financial stress or pressures
- Bullying or disempowerment
- Loss of a loved one
- Grief or sadness
- Emotional abuse
- Fear or worry

- Sleep deprivation or fatigue
- Depression
- Too many responsibilities
- No social connections or loneliness
- Guilt or self-blame
- Caring for aging or sick family members

You may come up with your own examples, but remember, everyone copes differently in one situation or another. A common example of the emotional eating cycle would be if you had the overwhelming responsibility of completing a large task at work by the end of the day. You may notice your heartbeat racing, your adrenaline pumping, your anxiety levels peaking and your mind fluttering from one thing to another. To end your day you grab a large order of fries that are heavy on salt at the drive-thru in order to bring your mind and emotional levels back to normal. If this is your *usual* work day, you have to understand that this coping mechanism is going to bring negative health results.

The first step is to put in a "stress modifier" when your emotions or moods start to peak or plummet. A stress modifier is something you put in place for yourself in order to stabilize your feelings. An example for the previous situation would be to ask a loved one for a big, long hug when you walk in the door or sit in a dimly lit room and breathe deeply for five minutes. These may sound too simple to have any real beneficial results, but they will decrease your cravings as anxiety levels start to come down. For every negative hormone / emotion that goes up, there is a positive hormone / emotion that can bring it down.

Jot down self-care activities that are quickly accessible to be your stress modifiers. Stress modifiers should bring you pleasure, comfort or calmness.

Here are some ideas for stress modifiers:
- Have a warm bath with lit candles.
- Sit in a dimly lit room with a soft blanket and a cup of herbal tea.
- Listen to soft music and have a glass of wine.
- Hug your children, spouse or pet (even if you don't feel huggy).
- Buy fresh-cut flowers and smell them.
- Watch videos on YouTube that make you laugh.
- Phone a supportive friend who is witty and funny.
- Ask a co-worker for a coffee or after-work drink to debrief or vent.
- Have a hot bowl of soup.
- Stretch to soft music.
- Give yourself a pedicure or better yet, get one done!
- Put a warm heat bag on your shoulders and breathe deeply.
- Nap.
- Walk around the block twice to wear off the adrenaline.
- Play an instrument (if you play one).
- Have sex or make out with your partner/spouse.
- Read a magazine and have a cup of tea in a real china cup.
- Ask your little one to rub lotion in your hands.
- Sit in the direct sunlight for fifteen minutes.
- Walk around in your bare feet in the grass.

_____

_____

_____

_____

Having a plan in place when you know stressful events will be coming your way in the near future is a sure way to keep you from diving into the snack cupboard because "management skills and well planned solutions for stress are the very heart of preventing downward spirals." *(Retraining the Brain, Dr. Frank Lawlis, 2009)* As a working mother, coming home and running a bath may not be an option. Therefore, be realistic but be determined to follow through, even if it seems a little inconvenient to others. Putting yourself first every now and then isn't going to bring detrimental effects to your family. In fact putting yourself last all the time will affect your emotional health and morale.

Having a method planned out is key since, once the pressure strikes, the last thing you are feeling is creative energy to come up with something to make you feel better. You can break the cycle of emotional eating; however it requires knowing your triggers and how to take care of yourself: awareness, planning and action.

Relax with a cup of tea

Herbal teas are relaxing and soothing to the spirit and should be part of our stress-coping strategies. Teas are not only beneficial to our health but also effective for psychological stresses. There are many flavors of teas for specific symptoms such as chamomile tea which is used for restlessness, anxiety, or stomach cramps. Researchers are discovering that teas have healing benefits as the plant nutrients are fueled with flavonoids. Flavonoids have an antioxidant function that means they are capable of mopping up and deactivating potentially harmful free-radicals which, if left to roam the body, can spark chronic health problems. In the traditional Chinese culture drinking tea is incorporated in their daily lifestyle as Chinese herbalists have long revered the healing properties of tea.

There is a great deal more to tea than its role as a refreshing beverage. So relax in knowing that your cup of tea not only smells and tastes great but is working to making you look and feel great.

Wash Your Worries Away Tea

2 Rooibos tea bags (any brand)
1 cinnamon stick
6 cups boiling water
2 orange slices
1 tsp honey or pkg of Stevia

Pour boiling water over ingredients in a large tea pot. Let steep for 3 minutes. Remove tea bags. Let sit for 5 minutes. To serve pour in a cup with a quartered slice of orange. Sip, savor, and slow down.

Tip: Drink your tea in the finest cup you own. You deserve it!

The power of breathing

How we take care of ourselves will determine our energy levels, vibrancy, confidence and lust for life. The issue is that we choose to put everything else before our own health interests which will cause a continual decline of our well-being. We seem to fall into the mantra "there just isn't enough time." But the *actual* truth is that small positive changes that take only five to ten minutes a day can promote miraculous results in just one month.

I wouldn't suggest anything I can't manage within my own day as I understand the (sometimes ridiculous) time constraints and overwhelming responsibilities life can bring. But this month I am going to ask you to try one thing that requires basically no physical effort and can be done anywhere and anytime. It has to do with your lungs.

Yes, it's breathing. Sure, this happens involuntarily and without much thought, however, we aren't REALLY breathing. Today we are shallow breathers. Our short rapid breaths are associated with stress and physical and mental tension. With chronic prolonged stress our lungs are not taking in the capacity they can hold which also can cause more physical and psychological stress. This natural act is becoming very unnatural, to the point we need to start consciously thinking about breathing, really breathing. **This trivial exercise of breathing can induce many benefits:**

- A deep slow breath can activate the release of tension, anxiety, and poisonous thoughts.

- Deep, relaxed breathing can reduce high blood pressure, elevated heart rate and risk of adrenal fatigue.

- Taking a deep breath in the face of conflict can help resolve a problem in a rational way.

- Deep breathing can reduce damage from stress and distress.

- Be a powerful tool to master more control of your emotions when combined with positive self-talk and thoughts.

- Help fight the urgency to use food to soothe and comfort.

To make this solution more powerful and effective remove yourself from stimuli into a quiet space for five to ten minutes. This will interrupt all your racing thoughts and allow a physiological and psychological "time-out". We need to give ourselves permission to stop and give something to ourselves. We don't have to fill every waking moment with a task because the truth is—it will NEVER all get done. And if it does we will probably just busy ourselves with a make-work project anyway. If we want to feel good and happy but we can't take five minutes for healing and self-care, then is it realistic we are going to achieve it?

Start being entitled to feel good and be free of all pressures of life for five minutes. Listen to your body and thoughts and if there is extreme tension then breathe. Deep within you there is clarity, strength, logic and healing—so breathe it out. We hold the destiny of what happens next and it can all start with that deeeeeep breath.

Reading food labels

Nutrition labels on food items list their ingredients in order by their amount. The best way to buy packaged food items is to choose those having only five ingredients or fewer, without artificial flavorings; or choose ones using organic ingredients. The worst foods to choose are those that have ingredients you can't pronounce or have sugars, sweeteners and enriched white flour. It is best to minimize foods that have listed: sugar, high fructose corn syrup, corn syrup, dextrose, brown sugar, maltose, modified corn syrup, corn starch, maple syrup, pear juice concentrate, maltitol and enriched or bleached white flour. This is especially so if sugars are one or two of the first three ingredients. These ingredients are hidden in over 100,000 every day products.

Products that state they are "fat free" usually mean that the fat was reduced but the sugar has been increased. "Sugar free" products use sweeteners and sucralose to replace sugar. These products still raise our insulin levels. This is especially detrimental to the health of diabetics or pre-diabetics. Using these foods during every meal will quickly add up to several teaspoons of sugar a day without seeing even one sugar grain. Labels can be deceptive on bread, cereal products and granola bars stating they are whole grain. In breads, look for other grains such as rye, millet, sprouted grains, wheat bran and flax. The best indicator is looking at how many grams of fiber are in the product; however, also be aware of how many grams of sugar a food contains per serving.

In summary:
- Look for under five ingredients or organic ingredients.
- Stay away from artificial flavorings.
- Pay attention to the first three ingredients.
- Look for sugar and sweeteners.
- Choose products with five grams or more of fiber per serving.
- Choose products with under five grams of sugar.
- Stay away from products with enriched/bleached flour.

A snapshot of the brain

- The human brain is the most complex organ in your body.

- The brain contains 100,000 miles of blood vessels.

- The brain is the organ of behaving and thinking. It determines how you think, feel, act, and interact with others.

- Basically it is WHO YOU ARE.

- Your soul is connected to your brain.

- The brain needs a constant, steady supply of glucose. It cannot store energy like your body does. "Without a constant supply from your digestive system and liver, delivered via your bloodstream, your brain would run short in about 10 minutes."
  (Prevention's, The Sugar Solution, 2006)

- The brain uses more calories than any other organ. In fact the more active our brain is, the more calories we burn.

- If you don't use it you lose it. Scans can show inactive parts of the brain. Injuries can also change your brain, therefore, change who you are. Long-term drug abuse also affects the brain by creating "holes" in it.

- When our brain is feeling sluggish, it requires another boost of glucose. This is why we feel more alert when we grab a sugary treat, pop, or a high-carb snack. Choosing foods with more nutritional value that gradually release glucose into the blood will sustain alertness and energy longer. "Blood sugar fluctuations profoundly influence your thinking over the short term and can alter the health of your brain and its ability to process and recall information over the long term." *(Prevention's, The Sugar Solution, 2006)*

- Carbs boost our serotonin levels and make us feel good. Healthy carbs are essential to help us relax and feel calm. Unhealthy carbs are commonly used to "self-medicate" or bring us comfort.

- The hormone, leptin, tells the brain how much fat is in the bloodstream and body. Leptin assists in regulating body fat. "When your body fat decreases, leptin levels in the blood fall sharply, telling your brain that the body needs more energy. These declining leptin levels trigger hunger and weight gain." *(Welcome to Your Brain, Sandra Aamondt, Ph.D. and Sam Wang, Ph.D, 2008)*

- The brain is the biggest influence on our metabolism. If our calorie intake goes down, eventually so does our metabolism. When we increase our calorie intake our metabolism eventually goes up, but not as fast as if we impulsively start bingeing. This results in rapid weight-gain. It is best to make healthier choices rather than to restrict calories. Making small gradual changes will ease your brain into a new pattern and help you to adjust to your new diet.

- Sugar spikes going up and down throughout the day can make us feel crabby one minute and happy-go-lucky another. Sugar changes our brain, therefore, changes our moods.

- Children with ADHD and ADD symptoms require a gradual, steady flow of glucose and should not be eating sugary and high-carb foods. This only increases the symptoms and makes it more difficult for them to concentrate. They require a good breakfast of whole grains and protein for learning at school ensuring stable blood sugar levels.

- Our Standard North American diet is becoming the major culprit for many mood and emotional disorders due to added sugars and sweeteners and reduction of vitamins and minerals.

- With today's pressures and stresses our brains demand more nutrients and amino acids in order to keep up with the demand of good-mood chemicals that help us cope.

- Good-mood enhancing brain chemicals are produced through a healthy diet of proteins, good fats and complex carbohydrates such as greens and vegetables. It is critical that these nutritional needs are met in order for the brain to function efficiently.

- Too much cortisol (your stress hormone) in the bloodstream on a regular basis will shrink your brain. Multi-tasking raises cortisol levels, therefore, chronic multi-tasking can shrink your brain. The hippocampus (memory part of brain) is damaged by stress. Brain decline can start as forgetfulness, dulled thinking and a decrease of positive emotions.

- Simply relaxing and thinking positive thoughts can help your brain repair itself by building new brain cells.

- Optimizing your diet with vital nutrients will protect and rebuild brain cells warding off mood disorders and brain diseases. Your brain health will define your quality of life.

We live in a world that places tremendous demands on our mental abilities. Our brain is continually trying to adapt to an ever changing, information-overload society. In order to cultivate a healthy mind we need to feed and treat it properly. Poor diet, stress, dehydration and lack of sleep contribute to poor mental stamina. Statistics for depression and dementia show increases every year displaying a trend in cognitive decline. Just about every step you take will influence your brain health, especially diet. If you are suffering brain fog or brain fatigue once or twice a day it is time you reassess your lifestyle habits. Your brain cannot be replaced or duplicated with anything else, so nurture it!

Grandma's cod liver oil

It seems grandma knew what she was talking about when she tried to make me take cod liver oil. There have been numerous studies from the past decade linking depression and emotional decline with low levels of Omega-3 fats that are only now becoming known to the general public. "A recent Australian study of 21 depressed patients confirmed that the most severely depressed had imbalances of fatty acids, mainly rock-bottom levels from fish oil, in their blood and cell membranes. Why? Evidence suggests DHA-type fish oil helps regulate serotonin, a neurotransmitter known for its "feel-good" qualities. Depressed persons often have low levels of serotonin." *(Your Miracle Brain, Jean Carper, 2000)*

Many of us removed fat from our diets in fear of gaining weight; however the right fats help preserve our health. Healthy fats are essential for efficient brain functioning. Our brains are made up mostly of fat and water and require fat to form new brain and nerve cells. Omega-3 fatty acids found in flax, seeds, olive oil, and fatty fish from cold waters boost moods and maintain a healthy brain. Our diet is becoming Omega-3 deficient; it's being replaced with unhealthy fats such as hydrogenated oils that interfere with the neurotransmitters in our brains. The neurotransmitters' primary role is to send messages from the brain to every system in the body including hormones. Hormones are strongly linked to our moods and emotional health. Therefore, good fats can bring forth clear thoughts and good moods.

Incorporating more healthy fats in the diet from foods such as wild salmon, sardines, farm eggs, ground flax, walnuts, dark leafy vegetables and free-range chicken decreases symptoms of depression and increases mental clarity. If Omega-3 foods are not easily accessible, it is recommended that a high quality fish oil such as wild salmon or krill oil is taken daily. Omega-3 supplements can also alleviate depressed moods and alcohol cravings. "Depression and cravings for alcohol, as well as fat, can usually be relieved by the use of supplements containing DHA from fish oil. No matter what your genetic background if you crave fats, try some omega-3 fish oil." *(The Diet Cure, Julia Ross, M.A. 1999)* If you experience the aftertaste of a fish oil supplement and it discourages you, try an enteric-coated fish oil capsule, which prevents fishy burps. Another method is to add Omega-3 oils or flax oil to your smoothie, over cottage cheese or as a salad dressing mixed with dried herbs.

Trans-fats are detrimental to brain health and must be eliminated from our diets. These artery-hardening fats alter the ability of neurons to communicate with each other and may cause degeneration of our mental health and learning abilities. Removing trans-fats and hydrogenated oils is not only important to good cardiovascular health but also vital to good brain health. Read labels to avoid hydrogenated or partially hydrogenated oils that clog up arteries and block neurotransmissions.

Try this smoothie as your morning snack. If you enjoy a smoothie for breakfast, complement it with a handful of walnuts or almonds.

Omega-3 Smoothie

1 cup	Greek yogurt
1/2 cup	pomegranate juice
1/2 cup	blueberries or sea buckthorn berries
2 tsp	flax oil or ground flax
1 tsp	ground chia seed
	half of an avocado

Optional: banana to sweeten

It's the hormones talking

When we speak about hormones we usually have "teenagers," "PMS" or "women" in the same sentence. We perceive hormones as controlling our moods or sex drive. Hormones play a much larger role than that. Hormones are very powerful in determining how we react to the world. "It is actually through the guidance of our hormones that the brain functions. Ultimately, these chemical messengers direct brain activity, impacting the development of traits that shape us as individuals."
(Feeling Fat, Fuzzy or Frazzled?—Richard Shames, MD and Karilee Shames, PhD, RN, 2005)

Understanding how our hormonal balance affects everything we do, think, and feel is the key to maintaining good health and preventing deterioration of our minds and bodies. Hormones are crucial to the proper functioning of all body systems. They tell our organs, cells and tissues what to do and when to do it. When our hormones are in balance (homeostasis), the results are amazing. We have energy, stable moods, a soaring sex drive and we feel and look vibrant.

However, we live in an ever-changing world with busy schedules and stressful moments. In order to maintain their balance our hormones react and adapt to everything we do—eating, sleeping, reading, driving, playing, daydreaming, etc. When life throws us a curve ball, our hormones change. Hormones play a primary role in helping us to bounce back easily from setbacks and they help us manage change. How hormones react can make or break your life: "hormonal stress can be as devastating to the brain's harmony as a vicious divorce." *(Retraining the Brain, Dr. Frank Lawlis, 2009)*

While the body is busy handling these stress-reducing tasks, all non-essential long-term processes are put on hold. Our body can only exist in one stage at a time: either growth, repair and building or protection mode. Let's take a look at the different hormones and their jobs.

Here are some examples beyond estrogen and testosterone that may surprise you:

Serotonin: This is a chemical in our brains that regulates our moods, emotions, memory, cravings, self-esteem, pain tolerance, sleep habits, appetite, digestion and body temperature. It is often referred to as the "happy hormone." It is the feeling we have inside when we have a new exciting experience. Chronic stress and multitasking are the two major serotonin suckers. Women are more at risk of low serotonin. When we are low on serotonin we tend to crave carbohydrates and sugar as they raise our serotonin levels. Ongoing stress can deplete our serotonin levels, which leaves us scrambling and grabbing sugary/high-carb snacks. This is one of the reasons weight gain and depression rates are skyrocketing. "The WHO projects that by the year 2010 depression and anxiety will be the number-one disability experienced by adults." *(The Hormone Diet)*

Dopamine: This is a brain chemical that influences well-being, alertness, attention, creativity, and concentration. It is the hormone that gives us pleasure and enjoyment from experiences such as eating chocolate and treats, surprises, exciting social experiences, exercise and love. Lacking dopamine will leave us craving more stimulation, which could put us at risk of addictions whether they are eating, sex or drugs. Dopamine can be one of the reasons why we are so dependent on foods to make us feel better. Stress also stimulates the production of dopamine in order to provide us with more energy and motivation. Stress can also give us the rush that can make some people addicted to drama and crisis. Addictive drugs as well as cigarette smoking and sugar produce dopamine. This is why smokers who try to quit smoking turn to eating sweet treats to replace the reduced dopamine.

Serotonin, **adrenaline** and **dopamine** are called *neurotransmitters*; they enhance or delay transmission of messages in the brain and nervous system.

Melatonin: This is a hormone that has two main jobs: it helps us sleep and repairs the body and brain cells. Melatonin is increased when the sunlight fades making us feel drowsy and sleepy. As we sleep (in darkness) melatonin is produced that repairs and replaces the damaged cells. Melatonin is also a powerful antioxidant and has anti-aging benefits. It increases our immune system and assists in the production of serotonin in order for us to look good and feel good. Melatonin also takes a hand in the production of appetite-suppressing hormones that keep us from over eating the next day.

Cortisol: This hormone is our coping mechanism that deals with both our immediate and chronic stress. Having too much stress in our lives or constant multi-tasking strips away this hormone. Cortisol is known to shrink and damage brain cells. Researchers starve lab rats to test the detrimental effects of stress. Skipping meals causes cortisol levels to rise, which makes us irritable. Cortisol is produced and stored while we sleep, which is why it's at its highest point in the morning and is drained throughout the day. If this hormone isn't replenished, concentration and memory are affected and the tired-but-wired sensation becomes a daily symptom.

Adrenaline: This is the stress reaction hormone. Adrenaline is excreted from the adrenal glands into the blood causing the body to be more efficient in "fight or flight." Adrenaline increases strength, raises heart rate and blood pressure, dilates pupils and redistributes blood flow from skin and inner organs. Glucose is rapidly directed to the muscles for energy, conditioning the body against the threat upon it. Type A personalities tend to be addicted by the adrenal rush, needing excessive activity to produce a "high." However, this stress response is supposed to be short term. After time your adrenal glands will go on strike and cortisol levels will tank, resulting in chronic fatigue, lack of stamina for exercise, more allergy symptoms, depression, sleep disruption, blood sugar imbalances, increased cravings and weakened immunity. Anxiety, jittery nerves, on-going excessive headaches and tense muscles are common symptoms of adrenal exhaustion. Adrenal fatigue is becoming more common and is often misdiagnosed as depression or anxiety.

Thyroid: The small butterfly-shaped gland found in your neck produces the thyroid hormone that has a profound effect on many of our physiological processes such as development, growth, fertility and metabolism. It is considered the "gas pedal" of our metabolism; therefore a deficiency called hypothyroidism can lead to weight gain, sluggish energy, low sex drive, very dry skin, cold intolerance and decreased blood flow to organs. Many people go undiagnosed with thyroid issues as few seek answers to these symptoms thinking they are normal.

If you struggle with weight gain and consider yourself one of those people who gain a couple of pounds just by looking at a piece of bread, then it's a good idea to seek out an endocrinologist or hormone specialist who can test your thyroid levels. It's important to follow up with your own research as well because it can still be difficult to pinpoint exact levels as the TSH blood test is not always accurate. Living with low or high thyroid levels decreases your quality of life and you shouldn't have to suffer needlessly. There are many written resources available addressing thyroid issues.

Cortisol, **thyroid** and **adrenaline** are the three hormones that, when out of whack, can cause havoc in our bodies resulting in illness and diseases including mental disorders. Constantly over-producing cortisol and adrenaline day after day because of ongoing stress and multi-tasking, skipping meals, excessive calorie reduction and insufficient carb intake, too much protein consumption, high and low blood sugar, lack of sleep or too much coffee will lead to adrenal burnout, cortisol depletion, and simple shut down.

What's important to remember is that our hormones all interact with one another; therefore if one hormone is off kilter it will cause a domino effect on the others. For example, if your adrenal glands are depleted of adrenaline your thyroid will kick in double time trying to replace the missing hormone, eventually overwhelming the thyroid.

Today many people are suffering from chronic stress. In time this wear and tear on the hormones starts to show. Cortisol, adrenaline, estrogen and insulin start to deplete causing some of these symptoms:

- rundown immune system
- foggy thinking
- memory lapses
- aches and pains in joints
- unstable moods, including depression and anxiety
- loss of energy
- loss of sex drive
- weight gain
- cravings for salt and sugar
- insomnia
- premature aging

- bloating
- acne
- feeling wired or shaky

If you have these regular symptoms you need to start becoming aware of what is going on in your life that is activating your hormones. What are they trying to adapt to or what is causing you to be stressed? Hormonal health depends on nutrition, adequate sleep, maintaining muscle, stress-management, and avoiding toxins and medications. Hormones are key to sustaining good health and energy under constant pressure and helping us to manage and cope with all of life's circumstances. These hormonal resources ensure our resiliency and good mental health. Disregarding the importance of nurturing them will end in weight gain, fatigue and misery. Be part of the plan instead of having a plan forced on you!

"The adults of the last four generations have blessed our children with the destiny of a shorter lifespan than their own parents . . . because of the landscape of food that we built around them."

Jamie Oliver (speech from TED.com)

Adrenal fatigue: a growing condition

Are you one of the thousands of people who have gone to a doctor with lackluster energy, low moods and drive only to be passed off as being mildly depressed? Were you prescribed medications for your depressed moods to feel only slightly better? Well, I'm here to tell you about a possible misdiagnosis of depression and introduce you to another mood disorder in town that not many people know or talk about.

Adrenal fatigue is rarely diagnosed, however, is a growing problem due to chronic stress and poor diet. Those suffering with adrenal fatigue tend to feel anxious, depressed, confused, less tolerant, powerless and easily frustrated. They hate mornings and perk up after supper. They feel overwhelmed and out of control. They use coffee, sugar and alcohol for energy and comfort, and suffer low blood sugar symptoms such as the jitters and brain fog.

The adrenal glands excrete hormones that are used in a fight-or-flight situation, however, in today's world they assist us in coping with life's upsets and demands. These hormones help us respond well in a crisis and help us be resilient to all the stressors that come our way.

But difficulties will arise when there is no recovery period: "The prolonged state of stress causes the adrenal cortex or outer layer of the adrenal gland to become enlarged, important lymph nodes to shrink, and the stomach and intestines to become irritated. The adrenalin system eventually "crashes" and forces the victim into a state of prolonged and severe fatigue." *(Adrenalin and Stress, The Exciting New Breakthrough That Helps You Overcome Stress Damage, Dr. Archibald D. Hart, 1991)* Stress management is essential to a healthy adrenal system and most importantly your emotional health.

Adrenal fatigue suffers usually have been bombarded with a large stress load or experience stressors one after another with little reprieve. It may be that marital issues, stressful workplace, caring for aging parents or financial issues start depleting your adrenal glands, then the next stressor like your car getting written off in a car accident becomes the straw that breaks the camel's back. By the time you are experiencing adrenal fatigue, your body has used up all the stored nutrients and is in desperate need of a new supply.

Our current North American standard diet is lacking the essential nutrients required to recover from stress, which is why it's important to eat highly nutritious foods. Food is the beginning and the sustaining element of adrenal recovery. If you have adrenal fatigue, when you eat is just as important as what you eat. Skipping meals and dieting also puts strain on your adrenal glands. Keeping blood sugar levels stable also makes a difference in mental stamina and body energy. Low blood sugar drains our stress hormones. Those with adrenal fatigue usually rely on caffeine, chocolate, energy drinks and high sugar foods to keep them stimulated and awake, however the destructive blow of a sugar crash or the rise of cortisol levels from a large dose of caffeine only makes the situation worse.

Nutritional supplements can assist in your body to recover and heal at a more rapid rate. Vitamin C is a very helpful supplement and should be taken daily if you are under a lot of stress. Food is the foundation of health repair and healing and cannot be emphasized enough. Adrenal hormones not only help us cope with stress but influence our overall health. Autoimmune diseases, allergies, and low thyroid function are also linked to under-functioning adrenal glands.

Our lifestyle also needs to be addressed in order to allow recovery to happen. Sleep deprivation, excessive exercise, demanding schedules and unresolved re-occurring issues eventually bankrupt our adrenal glands putting our mental and emotional health at risk. Sleep is one of the fastest methods to heal and restore our adrenal glands.

Unfortunately by the time adrenal fatigue sets in our sleep patterns are disrupted and sleeping through the night is a rare occurrence. When adrenals run high, sleep falls short. The condition worsens and anxiety becomes more profound and if we continue to abuse ourselves. Adrenal exhaustion can ultimately lead to panic attacks and heart palpitations. The symptoms can become quiet severe if one is not serious about making a decision to start dialing their life down.

If you feel you may be over-stressed, suffer from chronic flus and colds, get easily frustrated over the slightest annoyances, have difficulty crawling out of bed and suffer low moods and energy, maybe your adrenal glands need an overhaul. Please take the time to research adrenal fatigue as is it is now being written about and acknowledged as an actual condition. The adrenal glands may be small but they play a huge role in our health and we need to start taking care of them to take care of ourselves.

Pump up that love hormone!

Make today the perfect time to pump up your love hormone levels to help reduce food cravings and ease stress. Oxytocin is commonly dubbed the "love" hormone or "cuddle" as it plays an important role in reproduction and relationships. It is secreted by the pituitary gland in our brain and can easily be activated, providing many health benefits.

Oxytocin is the hormone that gives us sexual arousal, helps us form attachments, protect and breastfeed our young, and foster generosity and empathy. It is a good-mood hormone that feels good and promotes bonding and connecting. Oxytocin is activated by the sensation of a warm touch or nurturing. It is a built-in system that helps us connect, form communities and have a sense of responsibility towards each other. This good-mood hormone has many physiological and psychological benefits. Oxytocin can counteract the negative consequences of the bad-mood hormone, cortisol. Although it has its importance in the hormonal system, cortisol, the stress hormone, can put our physical and mental health at risk if levels are chronically elevated. Oxytocin has the ability to calm us down, slow our breathing and reduce our blood pressure, which enables us to manage stress more effectively. This is helpful to those who turn to food or alcohol to relax, comfort and soothe raw or wired nerves after a tough day. It can also be comforting for those suffering with anxiety or pain.

There are natural methods to induce oxytocin such as hugging, kissing, touching, or talking with someone you care about. A ten-second hug while breathing deeply will instantly reduce your blood pressure. Even looking fondly at a picture of a loved one can bring on a flow of oxytocin. Oxytocin is not only for people who have partners or family members at their disposal. Social networking, playing with a pet, dancing, singing and praying can also raise oxytocin levels. Volunteer work and donating to a charity close to your heart also assists in producing oxytocin.

Religion and spirituality can also awaken mellow oxytocin levels by feeling grateful for all the blessings you have received. Feelings of gratefulness breed happiness and well-being. Also connecting with a higher being brings forth feelings of purpose and meaning which generates good-mood chemicals. Rick Warren, a pastor of the Saddleback Church, devised a get-healthy plan with his congregation which attracted media attention and resulted in being featured on the Dr. Oz show. The community support and love of God and one another has created powerful benefits for the Saddleback members.

The benefits of oxytocin are being recognized so much that a nasal spray has been designed to instantly spike up levels. Oxytocin is being used for improved sleep, enhanced memory, stress-management, impotence, increased healing, pain relief and reducing blood pressure and cravings. We have the ability to produce our own natural oxytocin so put love and attention into your relationships so you can feel good, manage stress and reduce food cravings.

Does stress really make us fat?

Stress can be a good thing. It can save your life, help finish a project, and force you to make a decision. Stress is induced by triggers or fears that are helpful on a short-term basis. An example would be if you are driving on the highway and you blow a tire. The trigger is the loud pop and your car veering out of your lane. Your stress response hormone, adrenaline, allows you to instantly recognize danger and helps you safely roll onto the side of the road in mere seconds. After you sense danger is out of the way, your heart rate and anxiety levels start to stabilize and adrenaline is no longer gushing through your body.

Now you are left with the aggravation of having to change the tire, which is more of a hassle than dangerous. Your stress response hormone, cortisol, now rears its head as it provides you with motivation to solve a problem or face an issue because it feels unpleasant and you want it to go away. Once the tire is changed and the problem is solved, you drive off feeling a sense of relief that the crisis is over and cortisol is no longer required. After this experience a recovery period for your stress hormones is required, therefore, you may feel fatigued with the need of a rest. You may also experience cravings because blood sugar is low and brain chemicals are reduced. Most people report craving sugar during this stage as it is a quick way to recover from the stress and low energy.

Now this is all fine and dandy if we encounter these situations once or twice a month as they can be easily managed. However, in today's fast-paced world that's not the case. We are bombarded by stressors on a regular basis, whether it's our environment, workplace, relationships, financial situation, social issues, or all of these. After some time our normal coping mechanisms start to break down and our hormone levels are completely out of whack. Chronic stress and chronic multi-tasking will result in physical and psychological consequences.

It has been discovered that chronic stress compromises our immune system, damages brain cells and strains our cardiovascular system. This potentially can result in regular bouts of cold and flu, "foggy thinking" and increased risk of cardiovascular disease. Prolonged stress also causes disruptions in our digestive systems. Have you ever been so nervous that you ended up with diarrhea or ulcers? Psychologically we come to feel that we will never overcome all of our problems or complete all our responsibilities. This overwhelming sense of feeling out of control will result in burn out, anxiety or depression.

Our hormones play a key role in how well and how long we can cope with all the stressors we are faced with. Our hormones continually adjust themselves to help us through whatever task is at hand. Eventually, our hectic lifestyles cause hormonal havoc-bringing symptoms to the surface. "Chronic elevation in cortisol, day after day after day, also breaks down muscle and bone, slows healing and normal cell replacement, and impairs digestion, metabolism, and mental function, among other things." *(The Hormone Makeover, Donna White)* It is important to acknowledge these symptoms as we tend to drudge on, ignoring the small warnings our bodies give us.

The overload of the hormone, cortisol, will interfere with the functioning of other hormones which will become noticeable through moodiness, decreased energy and insomnia. Hormonal imbalance not only results in unstable moods or behavior changes but also weight gain. Anyone with a thyroid issue can understand the battle with weight management. Cortisol overload also contributes to weight gain as it triggers appetite and cravings for carbs and sugary treats. "Cortisol also sends a potent signal to abdominal fat cells (those in your belly region) to store as much fat as possible—and hold on to it." *(The Cortisol Connection Diet, Shawn Talbott. Ph.D)*

The foods we crave to ease our stress and bring us comfort are usually the ones that are the worst for us in terms of weight gain and digestive issues. Physical activity assists in weight loss and promotes positive moods, however an on-coming headache from being so overwhelmed or fatigued will prevent any treadmill attempts.

As our happy hormone, serotonin, dips we feel our mental stamina and moods bottom out. This leads us to seek ways to bring ourselves back to life. The first and most convenient method is through food. However, with our cortisol level high and serotonin low, we don't have the energy for self-control or rational thinking about food. Running into this situation daily it's easy to understand how weight gain can start to become an issue.

We must also keep in mind that sometimes stress is self-generated. Not every little annoyance or obstacle is a catastrophe. Worst-case scenarios rarely happen, therefore we need to realize that extreme anxiety or worry is detrimental to our health and physiological state and probably not helpful to the situation either. If you are feeling that almost everything now is causing a higher-than-normal strength stress response, you could be dealing with an exhausted or depleted hormone. Fortunately hormones are now getting more attention from physicians and health practitioners. Be sure to consider seeking the advice of a medical professional who is more in tune with how you "feel" and not just interested in your list of symptoms.

Lifestyle habits, self-care techniques and diet are essential in managing stress. The good news is that we do have the tools in our grasp to bring back balance to mental and emotional health. Bringing some harmony back into your life is an important part of weight loss and the first step can be as easy as sitting in your backyard by yourself for ten minutes to calm your mind. The quality of food also plays a significant role in managing stress and strong emotions. There are foods that deplete your good brain chemicals and raise cortisol levels.

Sugar, not so pure

Most people are well aware that sugar is not very good for them. Then why has the rate of consumption doubled over the last ten years? North Americans are sugar-consumers: "The average American consumes 149 pounds of refined sugar each year. If your body were to convert this, it would add 79 pounds of fat." *(Dr. Bob's Guide to Stop ADHD in 18 Days, Dr. Robert DeMaria, 2005)* Soft drinks are also becoming part of our daily diet and are beginning to replace water, our natural drink for cleansing and rehydrating. Many of my weight-loss clients are reporting that they have difficulty drinking pure water without flavoring or sweetness. Our chronic dependency on sugar will bring forth many diseases. Understanding through experience the negative effects of sugar on our bodies may not be immediate, as it takes years for a disease to manifest. Emotionally and mentally, however, the effects are felt at once when we try to get ourselves off sugar.

Sugar is an acceptable social addiction. North Americans are caught up in a deep emotional eating cycle with sugar. "Continuing use despite adverse consequences is the formal definition of addiction. Your mood is bad, but you keep on eating bad-mood food." *(The Mood Cure, Dr. Julia Ross, 2002)* Many people use sugary drinks in order to get through a difficult task or day. Over time we become reliant on sugar to function.

Sugar can immediately increase your energy and elevate your mood because it goes directly from your mouth to your bloodstream. This is a temporary state of comfort as the pancreas is given the signal to gush insulin in order to bring the high blood sugar levels down. This is when you feel the "sugar crash" coming, deflating your energy and mood. As we become irritable, sleepy or tired, the thought of sugar-filled foods becomes our solution. This cycle can happen two or three times a day, straining your mental and physical health and throwing all systems out of balance. This gripping and vicious cycle is very difficult to give up. However it is necessary to wean yourself off sugar in order to obtain a healthy state of well-being.

Refined sugar and sugar substitutes have a powerful effect on our moods and bodily functions. Processed sugar is stripped of any nutritional value; therefore it does not contain minerals or vitamins and cannot be digested efficiently. Its lack of nutrients causes our bodies to rob the vital nutrients from organs in order to deal with the sugar. Consuming sugary foods is counter-productive as it prevents stored nutrients from being used where they are primarily needed in order to function efficiently, mentally and physically. Chronic sugar consumption exhausts the pancreas as insulin is demanded many times a day responding to the dramatic rise of sugar in the blood. "This surge often lowers blood sugar too much, causing fatigue, irritability, depression, mood swings, memory problems, confusion, and low libido as cells are deprived of fuel." *(The Hormone Makeover, Donna White, 2010)*

Insulin is also considered the "fat storage hormone" as it tells the body to store fat. Excess insulin in the body disrupts the balance of other hormones. Removing this one food item from your diet will stabilize your hormones and level out many chemical imbalances creating a healthier functioning body and mind. The list of health problems that are associated with sugar is enormous. I suggest taking five minutes to research the negative effects on the internet and you will be shocked at all the diseases linked to sugar, especially cancers. Reducing your sugar intake is one of the most productive steps you can take towards a disease-free and brain-healthy life.

Quick sugar facts

- 50 percent of teenagers consume a soft drink a day increasing their chances of obesity by 60 percent.

- Soft drinks have 8–10 teaspoons of sugar.

- Popular energy drinks have 12–16 teaspoons of sugar.

- Many food products marketed as "healthy" are full of sugar.

- Fruit juices are heavily consumed by children and are full of sugar.

- Today kids are eating 34 teaspoons of sugar a day. *(MSNBC.com)*

- Nearly 40% of children's diets come from added sugar and unhealthy fats.

- Sugar is the most common addiction in North America.

- Sugar and sugar substitutes were found to be 4 times more addictive than cocaine. *(2007 French study)*

- Processed and refined sugar contributes to obesity and obesity-related diseases.

- Processed sugar devastates your immune system and promotes inflammation.

- Sugar is hidden and added in over 10,000 products.

- The food and beverage industry targets children with excessive junk-food marketing.

- 50–75 percent of U.S. cold cereals contain sugar.

- Removing sugar from your diet will bring forth withdrawals as it is an addictive substance.

"You start with a whole grain, but then you process it, you strip it of anything that slows down eating. You add reinforcing substances, you add sugar to it. You add other stimuli to it, you make it into a habit. You add the emotional gloss of advertising, you add toys to it. You make it part of your routine. You make it something that is socially acceptable."

Dr. David Kessler on breakfast cereals.
"The Foods That Make Billions, The Age of Plenty", BBC Documentary.

Break the sugar habit

#1 Stop or reduce soft drinks (diet and regular)

Soft drinks are strongly linked to obesity and diabetes. If you are trying to lose weight and drinking soft drinks daily, you are sabotaging any progress. Look up the Soft Drink Challenge on YouTube to stop your soft drink addiction.

#2 Artificial sweeteners are not the solution

Artificial sweeteners actually cause an increase in sugar cravings and hunger.

#3 Stop bringing junk food home

If it's not in your cupboards, it won't be in your mouth. Yes, it's disappointing when you are tearing up the house looking for a treat. So try bringing home other alternatives such as pita chips, popcorn kernels, or dark chocolate.

#4 Reach for fruit when craving sugar

North Americans are addicted to sugar. Tapering off from sugar is going to be a difficult transition. To help you through those sugar cravings, grab fruit. Fruit has a natural sugar that doesn't spike up your blood sugar as quickly as sweet treats. An added bonus are the vitamins and nutrients you receive from fruit.

#5 Exercise

Everyone knows all the benefits from exercise and unfortunately there are no other substitutes. Ten minutes of exercise a day is better than none. Your blood sugar requires exercise to keep your sugar levels stable.

#6 Stop associating foods with emotions

People associate foods with emotions such as happy and sad. What is the most detrimental to children is when parents show them love by buying them sugary treats. An example would be at Christmas or Valentine's Day.

#7 Getting off the sugar is not going to be a cakewalk

Sugar withdrawals are going to be ugly. Headaches, tiredness and lack of energy will be the hardest to go through. Your body has relied on sugar for years and it's going to scream for sugar. If cold turkey is not an option, go week-by-week tapering off your intake. Your body will eventually balance the intake of sugar that it is now receiving and the cravings *will* decrease.

#8 Off the sugar? Awesome! But remember …

Now that you have dramatically reduced your sugar intake and your body is no longer requiring it, you need to try to stay committed. Christmas time, vacations and social events are usually filled with sugary treats and it will only take a couple of times for your body/brain to remember how it relied on sugar. In terms of addiction, this is like an alcoholic falling off the wagon.

> " I want people to say, 'I didn't know I was feeling so bad until I started feeling so good'."
>
> Mark Hyman, M.D.

The skinny on fat free and sugar free

We can walk down any grocery aisle and find a number of products advertising they are "low fat", "fat free" or "sugar free." Over the last decade products have been popping up every year using this trend of making consumers believe they will help them lose weight; however, diabetes and obesity rates are still skyrocketing out of control. The reasons are:

- Fat in food makes us feel full and satisfied sooner.
- Fat releases the hormone, leptin, telling your brain you are full.
- Fat sustains us longer than low fat or no fat.
- Fat-free products use more sugar to ensure the product is still tasty and appealing. Example: flavored yogurts
- Sugar in foods spikes up our blood sugar sending a surge of insulin through our bodies.
- Insulin tells the body to store fat; the more insulin is produced the more our bodies store fat.
- Artificial sweeteners are used for "low-calorie" foods that increase cravings and appetite and still may cause the pancreas to release insulin.
- Consumption of diet soda increases your chances of obesity more than regular soda.
- Brown sugar is not healthier than white sugar. It just has molasses added to it.
- Stevia is known not to raise insulin levels. In Japan, Pepsi soda beverages are already using Stevia. It is not yet approved as a food but is as a supplement. Stevia can be grown in a herb garden.

Insulin, more than diabetes

Most people associate the word insulin with a diabetic, as someone who lacks the release of insulin to stabilize blood sugar. It has been discovered in the past few years that insulin is a hormone that boosts memory. Insulin is not just something that we require in order to not feel jittery or faint after digesting a frosted doughnut. Snacking or eating does stimulate the brain's activity as the brain does not store energy and so it needs a steady supply of glucose.

This glucose comes from the food we choose, "But some foods aid insulin's brainwork, and the trail leads to Omega-3 fats, found in canola oil, and fish such as salmon." *(Psychology Today, "Ups and Downs and Ins(ulin)", February 2010)* If you are one of those people who reach for a sugary pastry when feeling sluggish, you are not alone. However, this sugar-spike response only supplies the brain with glucose for a short time, soon leaving your brain feeling cloudy and drained again. Consuming a meal or snack of more complex carbohydrates such as whole grains, fruits and vegetables will result in more positive and longer-term effects.

Continuing research on insulin and memory has revealed new evidence that Alzheimer's disease may be a higher risk for Type 2 diabetics who struggle with blood sugar levels and in insulin resistance. "Evidence has shown that brain cells need insulin to survive and that a drop in brain insulin levels leads to brain cell damage." *(Diabetes Drugs Protect Against Alzheimer's-Related Memory Damage, WebMD Health News, Feb. 2, 2009)* Alzheimer's is dubbed by some as Type 3 Diabetes as studies show that many suffering from Alzheimer's have pre-diabetes or Type 2 Diabetes. It is apparent that the hormone, insulin, plays a significant role in cognitive ability.

Chronic release of insulin into the blood has its negative consequences. Not only does it put excessive demand on the pancreas to produce insulin but it also causes stress on the body. Too much insulin will trigger a rise in the hormone, cortisol, the stress hormone. Chronic high levels of cortisol in the system are dangerous and destructive.

Insulin also gives messages to the body to store fat. Therefore, eating sugary foods causes weight gain. Even "sugar-free" foods using artificial sweeteners cause insulin to be released because the sweet taste may initially trick your brain into believing sugar is being ingested. Excess insulin also disrupts leptin, our satiety hormone, putting us at risk of leptin resistance. If we cannot sense when we are becoming full, we will overeat. Insulin resistance and pre-diabetes are true warning signs that you are putting your hormonal and brain health at risk. Maintaining stable blood sugar is imperative to weight management, hormonal health and mental well-being.

In summary, choosing foods that are not high in glucose and eating regularly will increase your brain's activity and provide long-term benefits throughout the day. Healthy eating, healthy brain.

What's your fix? Sugar or salt?

When a food craving hits, some people prefer sweet treats like cookies or sweet pastries, while others seek out salty snacks like potato chips or French fries. What many people are not aware of is that most processed foods contain both. The mixture of sugar and salt has a powerful influence on our appetites and can lure us into a shark-like eating frenzy. For instance, a cheesy snack cracker would obviously taste salty; however the hidden sugar is so subtle that though you wouldn't taste it, your taste buds and brain can register it. Soda drinks also contain salt, however the sugar overpowers the salt, making us unaware of its existence.

What does salt do? It makes us thirsty causing us to drink more soda. This mixture in foods also stimulates your appetite encouraging you to eat more and that causes overeating. This engineering of a salt-sugar mix causes you to consume more calories resulting in weight gain.

If this sugar-salt combination isn't tempting enough, try adding fat and you have another whole mine field to get lost in. The fast food industry uses sugar, salt and fat in most of its menu items. "The food industry bombards our taste buds with a staggering variety of flavors. These companies have processed sugar, salt, and harmful fats into foods that no longer bear any discernible resemblance to their origins." *(The Flavor Point Diet, David L Katz, 2005)* Anyone could easily fall prey to a fast food addiction as this tempting mixture tantalizes any craving whether it is sugar, salt, or fat. The fast food giants are well aware of the temptation of flavors and use many carefully designed flavor mixtures and additives to keep customers coming back.

Fast Food Nation author Eric Schlosser exposes how fast food companies use a cocktail of flavor chemicals to hook in their customers. "The flavor industry is highly secretive. Its leading companies will not divulge the precise formulas of flavor compounds or the identities of their clients." *(Fast Food Nation: The Dark Side of the All American Meal, Eric Schlosser, 2001)* Additives, flavorings and sweeteners are added to over stimulate your tastebuds and certain brain curcuits ensuring you will come back for more. The manipulation of flavors is the major culprit of fast food addictions resulting in high obesity rates. If you walk into a fast food restaurant, you are better off to order just the coffee, black.

In order to decrease your sugar or salt craving start weaning yourself away from over-processed and refined foods. Including more wholesome, home-cooked foods where sugar and salt can be controlled is a good start. Also, if you have a salt craving then choose a salty food such as a cucumber with sea salt. If you have a sweet tooth, try a fruit salad or home-baked cookie. Do not combine the two or your craving will not be satisfied but confused and stimulated. If you continue the trend of eating whole foods you will find that your taste buds will change, requiring less and less sugar and salt. The biggest advantage of feeding your cravings this way, aside from losing weight, is that you will begin to prefer more nutrient-dense foods providing your body and mind with the fuel they need to heal, balance and function efficiently.

Feeding your happy hormone

Serotonin is a hormone that is found in the brain, digestive tract, and platelets. It is commonly described as the "happy hormone" as it greatly influences positive moods. In addition to regulating moods, serotonin plays an important role in appetite, sleep, sexual drive and controlling body temperature. We require adequate levels of serotonin for our overall well being. This important hormone will help you stay alert, sexually active, motivated, optimistic, well rested and most of all, happy. Having low levels of serotonin will leave you feeling exactly the opposite, putting you at risk for depression.

Skyrocketing rates of depression show that it is becoming a widespread epidemic. We are becoming a "serotonin deficient" society and this is related to a toxic diet void of nutrients, lack of physical activity and chronic stress. Many people, looking for ways to pull out of this slump, turn to one tactic we seem to use on a regular basis: eating sugary, processed foods. These foods become addictive as they provide a temporary state of pleasure by quickly raising our serotonin levels. Serotonin is also an appetite suppressant, helping us know when to stop eating. This means that when we turn to unhealthy foods for a temporary pick-me-up and we have low levels of serotonin, we don't have the ability to stop eating. Soon after, we feel guilty or ashamed of about our bingeing fest. Once we start riding this merry-go-round it is very hard to get off. Therefore low serotonin levels are directly related to obesity and food addiction.

To avoid a serotonin deficiency it is important to follow a well-balanced diet that promotes digestive health. Your body relies on certain amino acids from proteins, primarily L-Tryptophan, in order to manufacture adequate levels of serotonin. Since your happy hormone is produced in your digestive system the "pipes" need to be working smoothly for adequate production.

It's not about willpower

Eating is a pleasurable experience. As adults we carry many favorable memories linked with food. We are all unique as to what foods we do and don't like, however most of us share the same taste for sugar, fat, and salt. We inherently desire these types of foods. Fat is needed to absorb fat-soluble vitamins and supply essential good fats for vital organ functions. Some fats contain Omega-3 fatty acids that prevent depressed moods and aging of the brain. The body requires sodium to regulate fluid balance and muscle and nerve function. Natural sugar provides emergency energy for tired muscles and a foggy brain. We mustn't try to eliminate these foods, but we do need to seek out healthy alternatives to junk foods.

A majority of people would say that food is the only thing that shuts down cravings. A craving is a message from the brain to fulfill a particular requirement for optimal functioning. The brain lets us know that there is a deficiency somewhere that needs to be replenished. Because the brain doesn't clearly tell us what exactly we need and where the levels are inadequate, we need to take a few minutes to pinpoint what is going on with our mood and how we feel physically. We need to work with the cravings and not against them. How many times have you tried avoiding your cravings by eating around them? You picked this and nibbled on that, later coming to realize you have eaten half the house out so you may as well have the bowl of chocolate ice cream. It's not about willpower or resisting temptation as the brain will not ease up on its demands until it is satisfied. You will not win.

To satisfy cravings without risking weight gain we need to choose higher quality foods instead of refined processed foods loaded with sugar and monosodium glutamate (MSG) as both raise insulin levels. The mental and emotional benefits of these foods are short term and promote further cravings. If you are craving fat then reach for good fats such as nuts, seeds, guacamole, eggs, almond butter and olive oil dressings. The more we choose healthier foods to satisfy a particular craving, the more we will decrease the intensity of further cravings.

If you choose to go with a not-so-healthy food option such as a processed food item, you need to be aware that it is designed to be seductive and addicting, encouraging you to keep eating. Try nibbling and savoring, enjoying the experience instead of wolfing it down. Remain in the moment and aware of how it is making you feel, psychologically. One thing is clear: In order to correct whatever deficiency there is, you must choose real foods that contain valuable nutrients and not junk foods void of nutrients. When incorporating healthier snacks you will eventually come to enjoy real foods, turning you away from damaging foods that rob you of your good moods and induce further nagging cravings resulting in weight gain.

Amino acids: Good for your mental health

Every cell in the body is comprised of proteins, the building blocks of life. Proteins are a necessary part of our cells as they provide the structure of all living things. Amino acids are the chemical substances that make up proteins. There are 22 amino acids to make up the 50,000 different proteins we must have to be healthy. Of the 22 amino acids there are eight that are essential for human nutrition. An essential amino acid cannot be synthesized or replicated, therefore it must be part of the diet. Amino acids enable vitamins and minerals to perform their jobs efficiently and inadequate supply can hinder synthesis and reduce healthy levels. The most common way to get amino acids into the diet is to eat quality foods such as high protein lean meats, fish, grains, leafy greens, nuts and low-fat dairy products. Amino acids play a significant role in raising levels of brain chemicals, helping us cope with stress, manage anxiety and multi-task efficiently. Four key mood chemicals are made of amino acids. If you are eating a proper diet, including plenty of protein (other than from meat), your moods are enhanced and cravings for comfort foods are suppressed. With the absence of proper good-mood fuel you may experience food cravings, dull moods, anxiety, obsessiveness, and lack of focus and mental stamina. "Many elderly people suffer from depression or neurological problems that may be associated with deficiencies of the amino acids tyrosine, tryptophan, phenylalanine, and histidine, and also of the branched-chain amino acids—valine, isoleucine and leucine." *(Prescription for Nutritional Healing, The A to Z Guide to Supplements, Phyllis A. Balch, CNC, 2008)*

Amino acids do have mental health benefits as some are needed for the brain to send and receive messages. A deficiency will bring on complaints of loss in mental stamina. A majority of people with this complaint end up reaching for refined carbohydrates, which will only bring short-term relief. This relief is rewarding at first, giving you pleasure and firing a temporary surge of endorphins. This is one of the reasons why foods seem so addicting; however amino acids would yield greater benefits.

Serotonin, known best as our key mood hormone, is made from an amino acid, L-tryptophan. Serotonin regulates our moods, emotions, memory, cravings, appetites, sleep patterns and body temperature. There are not many foods that contain tryptophan and if you are not eating a proper diet or worse yet, dieting, then serotonin levels become low. A drop in our serotonin level may result in feelings of low self-esteem, depression, fatigue, and obsessive or unclear thinking. With all the overwhelming pressures and tasks required from us daily, a low-serotonin brain is ill-equipped to handle stress and cope through the day.

Amino acids make up 75 percent of the body. They are essential to nearly every bodily function. Every chemical reaction that takes place in your body depends on amino acids and the proteins they build. There are essential and non-essential amino acids. Here are some examples of amino acids and their functions:

L-Glutamine—can stop or decrease sugar and carb cravings. It is also known as brain fuel as it increases the amount of GABA, which is needed to sustain proper brain function and mental activity. It also helps build and maintain muscle.

L-Theanine—can reduce stress and anxiety without tranquilizing effects.

Carosine—promotes healthy aging and protects tissues from the effects of glycation. Carosine levels in the body decline with age.

GABA (or gamma-aminobutyric acid)—induces relaxation, reduces stress and anxiety and increases alertness. It helps you feel more physically and mentally balanced.

Taurine—is needed for proper utilization of sodium, potassium, calcium and magnesium. It has a protective effect on the brain and has been used to treat anxiety, hyperactivity and poor brain function.

Vegetarians and vegans need to be wary of their protein intake. Many teen girls experiment with the vegan lifestyle in order to lose weight but end up eating a high proportion of carbohydrates and starches. It is important to visit a dietitian if you are radically changing your diet to ensure you are getting the right carbohydrate-protein combination. Essential amino acids are derived from our diet and not all proteins contain a sufficient amount. Supplementation can assist in deficiencies, however food is the best source. If you are considering a supplement form, please advise your health practitioner and ask questions of the health food store clerk. Health food stores carry an amino acid section. It is best that amino acids come from a natural diet; however if supplementing, it should not be for long-term usage. You can fully stock your brain with natural mood enhancers by eliminating simple carbohydrates and incorporating more protein.

L-tryptophan: elevating your mood

Tryptophan is one of ten essential amino acids that the body uses to synthesize the proteins it needs. It is well known for its role in the production of the nervous system's messages, especially those related to relaxation, restfulness, and sleep. It serves as a precursor for serotonin, a neurotransmitter that helps the body regulate sleep patterns, appetite, and moods.

Low levels of tryptophan may lead to low levels of serotonin. Low levels are associated with depression, anxiety, irritability, impatience, impulsiveness, inability to concentrate, weight-gain, overeating, carbohydrate cravings, poor dream recall and insomnia. Vitamin B6 is also necessary for the conversion of tryptophan to both niacin and serotonin. In addition, several dietary lifestyle factors that reduce the conversion of tryptophan are cigarette smoking, high sugar intake, alcohol abuse, diabetes and excessive consumption of protein. Tryptophan may play a role in the prevention and/or treatment of the following:

- anxiety
- depression
- headaches
- insomnia

- obesity
- obsessive compulsive disorder
- dementia
- Tourette's syndrome

Tryptophan is an all-natural food nutrient that is helpful with mood regulation. It has no side effects as do some anti-depressants, which also regulate moods. The best food sources come from protein: red meat, turkey, nuts, seeds, soybeans (non-GMO is best), tuna, shellfish, quinoa, duck, krill oil, eggs, beans, and lentils. Bananas also contain tryptophan. Feed your moods and fuel your life!

5–htp: low serotonin solution

Serotonin is essential for the brain, which is the control center for every physical function as well as our emotional and mental state. Each year depression, insomnia, obesity, migraines, and chronic fatigue rates are going up. Health experts are recognizing that our society is suffering from a disorder called serotonin deficiency syndrome. With this vital hormone being sapped from our brains by a hectic and stressed-out lifestyle, exacerbated by a too fast, junk-filled diet, our emotional and mental functioning is running on fumes. Not only does eating the wrong foods contribute to stress on our overall well-being but so does skipping meals, dieting, and consuming large meals at the end of the day.

Serotonin influences a wide range of behaviors including mood and eating patterns. Most diets fail because they wean out serotonin-producing foods causing serotonin levels to bottom out. If serotonin levels are not replenished this will promote the overeating of carbohydrates and sugary foods which lead to weight gain. Other consequences of serotonin deficiency include low moods, short attention span, intolerance, insomnia and dissatisfaction with life. The most severe impact of low serotonin can be the loss of drive or zest for life.

The restoration of serotonin is best done through a healthy diet, physical activity, and decrease of caffeine, alcohol, and physical and emotional stress. Eating more protein will help, but because of the brain-blood protective barrier not all tryptophan is filtered through. In fact, many amino acids are competing to get through to the brain, therefore an adequate supply of tryptophan may not always be possible. Fortunately there is a better way of overcoming serotonin deficiency quickly and that is 5-HTP. "The almost instant solution to most low-serotonin problems is an inexpensive nutrient supplement made from an African bean. It can be found in every health food store and many pharmacies in America. It's 5-HTP, 5-Hydroxy-tryptophan." *(The Mood Cure, Julia Ross, M.A., 2002)*

5-HTP is widely available without a prescription as it is considered a nutritional supplement. It has been used in Europe for over 30 years in treating depression, sleep problems, obesity and chronic fatigue. "While there are many questions yet to explore, the evidence is clear: 5-HTP is a safe, natural way to boost brain serotonin levels." *(Boost Your Serotonin Levels - 5-HTP. The Natural Way to Overcome Depression, Obesity and Insomnia, Michael Murray, N.D., 1998)* With many people struggling from low energy and sour moods due to lack of sleep, high stress, poor diet and constant weight gain, it is good news that there is a supplement available to boost our serotonin levels quickly.

People should question why this option is not broadcasted through the medical profession. However the answer is easily explained as 5-HTP cannot be patented by drug companies. Therefore there is no interest in researching, producing and marketing it. 5-HTP can be compared to garlic or Echinacea, as both have medicinal elements but cannot be patented. 5-HTP is not to be used long-term or with other anti-depressants. Please consult your physician in order to discuss the possibility of using this more natural way to manage depression. One side effect is nausea, which can be managed by taking it twenty minutes before eating. For insomnia, try taking one 5-HTP pill thirty to sixty minutes before bedtime. When used as part of a new healthier lifestyle that includes eating a balanced, natural diet, physical activity and stress management techniques, 5-HTP can help restore many areas of your life giving you the vitality you are seeking.

The fiber of life

We are sleep-deprived, stressed, dehydrated, inactive and constipated. If you do not have one bowel movement once a day you are indeed constipated. Constipation is the main cause of several acute and chronic diseases. Dietary fiber plays a significant role in the health of our digestive systems and we are not consuming adequate levels resulting in the disruption of many systems in our bodies.

The present intake of fiber by Canadians averages only from 4 to 11 grams a day. "The Canadian Guidelines state healthy adults should consume 26 grams of fiber a day" *(Canadian Diabetes Association)* Breads only contain one to four grams of fiber per slice. When humans relied on foods that came straight from the earth, we were consuming more than one hundred grams a day. We have replaced fiber with over-processed foods that contain none, or minimal fiber, as often the outer fiber layer of grains is removed. Fiber is extracted on purpose so the food can be preserved giving it a longer shelf life.

Fiber contributes to bowel regularity. Regularity should not be overlooked as impaired digestion can lead to a breakdown in physical and mental health. Constipation slows down the food in the intestines and harmful toxins begin to build up. If this becomes a chronic condition these toxins will end up being absorbed into the bloodstream, carrying them to different parts of the body and causing many serious health conditions. Foods that are fiber-rich not only help push things along but also mop up these toxins and carry them out of the body. You can determine your health by your bowel movements and their shape and size. Small, irregular stools can cause big problems!

Fiber also slows the release of glucose into your bloodstream. This helps in blood-sugar stabilization, therefore providing energy, decreasing appetite and improving mental clarity. Diabetics are recommended to increase their fiber intake in order to prevent blood-sugar spikes. This also allows your pancreas to stock up on insulin. By keeping blood-sugar levels consistently stable, one can prevent Type 2 Diabetes, lose weight, and improve brain function.

Some people find that increasing their fiber intake gives them discomfort and bloating, therefore discouraging them from staying on a high fiber diet. However, this effect is short-term as your digestive system will adapt. Boosting your water intake or taking a digestive enzyme supplement will assist in moving things along. Try adding more fiber to your cereal, yogurt, salads, and snacks. You will increase your chances of losing weight by looking for grams of fiber rather than calories on food labels. Your health also depends on it!

Love your gut

The digestive system is one of the most important systems in the body. It is responsible for digestion, transportation, absorption, and elimination of foods. The primary goal is to absorb nutrients in the foods in order to meet the needs of our cells, allowing all of our systems to function efficiently. Digestive enzymes play a significant role in this facilitation. Digestive enzymes are found in raw foods such as fruits, vegetables, greens, seeds and nuts. The body does have the ability to make digestive enzymes, however the body should only provide about fifty percent of the enzymes we need to digest food. The other half should come from raw or uncooked foods. The issue today is that the average person is not eating enough raw foods needed for our digestive systems to work effectively. This creates more demand on our organs, primarily the pancreas, to provide more enzymes. For our body to create enzymes it needs to draw energy and nutrients from other sources. Therefore, eating processed or refined foods becomes counter-productive. Blocked or slow digestion causes foods to ferment in our gastrointestinal tracts, which creates discomfort, bloating, gas, and sleepiness.

Quick Notes

- The digestive system absorbs nutrients from food.

- Our lifestyle and food choices put regular and consistent stress on our digestive systems preventing proper absorption of nutrients.

- The number one reason for indigestion is over-consumption of foods.

- Food should make us feel energized not bloated or sluggish.

- Scheduled eating or routines help the digestive system prepare for food by having digestive enzymes ready.

- Foods lose nutrients and digestive enzymes as they cook.

- All of our systems depend on digestive health.

- Improper digestion results in nutrient deficiencies putting us at risk for physical and mental illnesses.

- As we grow older we lose the ability to produce concentrated digestive enzymes.

- Weight gain is also a direct result of poor digestive enzymes. If the body is not receiving the essential nutrients it needs for vital bodily functions, the brain will keep telling us to eat.

- Food from a box usually has no digestive enzymes.

- Digestive enzyme supplements can be extremely helpful in resolving digestion issues.

- Pineapple and papaya are rich in digestive enzymes.

- Antacids are the number one over-the-counter medication because of indigestion issues.

If you suffer from regular indigestion or digestion symptoms, take note of whether you are eating any raw or uncooked foods. Try not eating processed or cooked foods for a week or take a digestive enzyme supplement before every meal to see if there is a noticeable difference. Digestive enzymes can be found at your local health food store. There are many to choose from so ask the health food store clerk what would be most helpful for your specific symptoms.

"The USDA (United States Department of Agriculture) is not our ally here. We must take matters in our own hands not only by advocating for a better diet for everyone—that's the hard part—but by improving our own diet and that happens to be quite easy. Less meat, less junk and more plants: It's a simple formula. Eat food; eat real food."

Mark Bittman, speech from TED.com

Toxins

We live in a very toxic and polluted world. All of us come into contact with toxins every day, which our bodies end up absorbing. Some toxins include:

- chemicals in plastic
- additives, coloring and flavoring
- prescription and over-the-counter drugs
- exhaust fumes
- heavy metals (some from tap water)
- air pollution
- household cleaners and chemicals
- skin care and makeup products
- steroids/hormones in some meats, depending on regulations

No matter how toxins get in our bodies, they do, and the accumulation of toxins starts to interfere with normal body functions. Some of the effects are weight gain, allergies and hormonal imbalance. Two of the most regular chemicals we are exposed to are Bisphenol-A (BPA) and phthalates that are most commonly found in plastic water bottles and other plastic food containers. Our natural purifying and cleansing systems include our kidneys and liver. However, with the abundance of toxins being absorbed (mostly through our skin), these organs are too overwhelmed, causing toxins to settle in our fat.

Chronic stress and lack of sleep also impede our systems' cleansing abilities. Eventually the results are weight gain, fuzzy feeling, mental and physical fatigue, lackluster skin, and allergies. More discoveries are being made during research that suggest that toxins cause cancer cells to divide faster making the cancer spread more quickly. "With all the cancer information and disinformation broadcasted continually through the major news media, rarely do we hear a mention of the greatest threat to our health - and the most prevalent cause of cancer: toxins." *(Cancer-Gate: How to Win the Losing Cancer War, Samuel Epstein, MD, 2005)* It is imperative that our countries' leaders take a stand against polluting our world and our health.

"In October 2009, Canada became the first country in the world to declare Bisphenol-A a toxic substance and to ban the importation, sale and advertising of polycarbonate baby bottles containing BPA."

Canadian Family Magazine, Winter 2009

Detox and purification

Cleansing your body of toxin blockage and build up is an easier process than you might think. Adding one or two changes to your lifestyle and diet will make an impact. If you continue adding another change every month, you will be fighting off illnesses more and more. Maintaining a strong detoxification diet long term is difficult; therefore doing a detox twice a year is recommended. Cleansing the body is a vital part of maintaining optimal health. *(See the full 10-Day Detox program on page 128)*. Otherwise, focusing on a few simple changes such as weeding out some foods and adding in others seems to be a method most people can manage.

- The USDA recommends half your plate be fruits and vegetables and Canada's Food Guide recommends seven to eight servings of fruit and vegetables. Seriously good recommendations!

- Choose antioxidant foods such as blueberries, pineapple, broccoli, beets, pomegranates, kale, green tea for maximum punch.

- Cut down red meat and eat more free-range turkey and wild fish. Stop saving turkey for Christmas time; it has significant benefits.

- Beans, beans, beans! High fiber foods clean out the system by absorbing toxins like a sponge and flushing them out.

- Drink eight glasses of water a day. Your kidneys need water to flush out toxins. Start with a glass at rising.

- Drink two cups of green tea a day.

- Don't microwave food, frozen dinners, or drinks in plastic containers.

- Use as many spices as you can; they have super antioxidant agents and natural medicinal benefits. Cinnamon is an easy one to use.

- Sweating is an excellent way to detox the body. People today are not sweating enough; therefore toxins are building up in our bodies, which will result in illnesses later in our lives.

- Go organic wherever you can, even if it's one or two items.

- Eight hours of sleep produces melatonin, which is a hormone that detoxes the body.

- Boost your Vitamin C, Vitamin E, and magnesium intake; they help with detoxing.

- Eat fewer processed and refined foods as they contain many chemicals and additives.

The liver: your body's detoxer

The liver is our detoxing organ. Everything we consume or absorb through our digestive and circulatory systems goes through our livers. The kidneys also help flush out toxins, however they need water to do so. If there is not enough water in the body (dehydration) then the liver has to kick in and help. This pulls the liver away from other important functions such as metabolizing fat and eliminating toxins. Therefore, drinking enough water helps in weight loss. In order to ensure the liver is clear and working efficiently we should consume less caffeine, alcohol, sugar and greasy foods.

It is imperative that the liver is working efficiently for weight loss to happen. If the liver is busy eliminating toxins then it cannot metabolize fat, which then remains stored in the body. Some people may only have half their liver working efficiently even without being heavy drinkers. Ultra sound technicians are finding fatty enlarged livers quite common. This is also regularly showing up in children whose livers have sometimes equated to the physical state of a fifty year-old man. Liver cleanses are used periodically to flush out all the matter that is clogging up the liver and interfering with its essential functions.

It is important to do a simple liver cleanse by sipping green tea with milk thistle or taking milk thistle supplements as you do the Ten-Day Detox. If you get tired of drinking water and tea for ten days, use only organic apple juice. The important part of a liver cleanse is to stay away from caffeine, alcohol, sugar, fatty, greasy foods, food additives and chemicals. For people working with chemicals that have strong odors, such as farmers, auto-body painters, industrial cleaners, and maintenance people, etc., it's recommended that you see your family physician to have your liver tested for its efficiency and health. Chemicals can be breathed in or absorbed through the skin (our largest organ).

Our liver plays a significant role:

- The liver secretes bile that aids in digestion of our food; without it digestion could not take place.

- The liver detoxifies the body; everything that goes through the digestive system and circulatory system goes through the liver.

- The liver acts as storage for numerous vitamins and minerals.

- The liver regulates the body's metabolism and metabolizes fat.

- The liver produces hormones and proteins that enable the body to grow and heal.

The recommendation is: Clean your liver, heal your body!

"Excessive weight is a symptom of liver dysfunction and not solely due to the number of calories you eat. We have been attacking the symptom of weight excess with fad diets, obsessional high-impact aerobic exerises, stomach stapling and toxic drugs such as appetite suppressants, laxatives and diuretics. We have failed to treat the underlying cause of liver dysfunction and indeed we have managed to virtually ignore the hardest working organ in the body."

Dr. Sandra Cabot, MD
The Liver-Cleansing Diet: Love Your Liver and Live Longer, 1996.

Food4thought **tidbits**

- Soup should be a staple in your diet (*look at the Chinese diet*).

- Try to cook with extra virgin olive oil or coconut oil.

- Add ground flax seed to your baking, smoothies and oatmeal.

- Eat five to six times a day with breakfast being your biggest meal.

- If it's white, don't bite—refined sugar and flours are harmful.

- Eggs got a bad rap: whites are full of protein and yolks are mood- boosters; if worried about cholesterol, eat egg whites.

- Green tea, chai lattes and dark chocolate are good for killing a craving.

- If you are one of the lucky ones who like olives, put them in and on everything you like! They're mood-boosters with good fat.

- Stock up on almonds, walnuts, pumpkin seeds, and hemp seeds.

- Use Sundays to cut up all veggies for the week and put them in baggies. Also make a BIG healthy salad for the week.

- Roast two chickens at once; for a side dish wrap 10 potatoes in foil and stick in the oven at the same time. You'll have multiple meals for the same amount of effort.

- Stop watching TV after 10 p.m.; you have nothing to gain except weight and more to lose, like sleep! This is when your body, mind and skin rejuvenate. Also, melatonin, serotonin and hormones are replenished during the night for good moods and low appetite.

- Stick the exercise equipment right in front of the TV for one month and you will find you have exercised more than last month.

- For night snackers, air-popped popcorn should be made every night and set out on the kitchen counter. Add a little butter or olive oil.

- Organic almond milk can be used to replace milk in baking recipes. Also tastes great in oatmeal.

- Put water in a clear container in the fridge with sliced oranges and lemons; it looks refreshing and kids will eventually drink more water. Or dilute the juice with water to decrease their sugar intake.

- Cook six or seven large chicken breasts and use for wraps, salads and pasta dishes. This will save time on three to five meals.

- If you want an alcoholic drink, choose red wine or vodka and tonic water or flavored water with a lime.

- Choose one organic item that is used regularly (*ex. coffee*).

- Ordering in a restaurant, you're better off to order two non-deep fried appetizers. Try a flat-crust veggie pizza and share.

- Boil six eggs and keep in the shell in the fridge for quick breakfasts.

- Use farm eggs and add spinach and feta when scrambling.

- Prepackaged pasta meals are full of fat, MSG and salt. Make your own and freeze.

- Introduce more home-cooked meals every month.

- Choose Stevia over sweeteners. Sweeteners increase cravings and appetite.

- Eat protein at breakfast and carbs at supper.

- Add tomatoes and cucumbers instead of only lettuce in sandwiches.

- Walk away from the TV during commercials; 90 percent are fast food and junk food commercials. Brains absorb these messages.

- For dessert have a homemade smoothie; it's better than ice cream.

- Put ground chia seed, cold green tea and blueberries in your smoothies; they are super foods with amazing antioxidants!

- When making rice (brown), throw in some barley or quinoa.

- Make a turkey every two months. It has tryptophan and lots of meal-making meat, making you feel good and saving you time!

- Toast whole wheat English muffins instead of white bread.

- Introduce sweet potatoes to your weekly menu. Kids love them.

- Have fresh herbs on hand to throw in salads, sauces and soups.

- Eating two to three apples a day will help you lose five lbs in six weeks.

- Plates have increased in size over the last 30 years. Ponder that.

- When making your own hamburgers put in chia seed and hemp seed.

- Anything with curry or turmeric is good for arthritis.

- Some fast food hamburgers and fries don't mold.

- Healthy breads mold within days, a good thing.

- Processed foods have no live digestive enzymes. Eat raw veggies.

- Sweat and sleep detox the body.

- Add beans and lentils to your weekly diet for much-needed fiber.

- Be wary of how many grams of sodium are in canned tomatoes.

- Choose frozen veggies over canned.

- Bruschetta can be used in many dishes and is very healthy.

- Try a new fresh herb like basil or cilantro in a dish.

- Sandwich meat, wieners and bacon have nitrates, which are very toxic.

- Barley is high in fiber and easy to throw into stews and soups.

- Dip bread in olive oil or butter it. It's healthier for you than dry.

- Toxins contribute to weight gain.

- Children will eat their own weight in toxins by age 18.

- Most medications contain toxins.

- Air fresheners and perfumes in chemical cleaners can activate histamines in the body.

- Reducing your toxic load will ensure better health.

- Sugar, wheat and dairy are common allergens.

- Reducing foods with gluten will gain you mental energy.

- Buckwheat is gluten-free and high in fiber.

- Inflammation is the root of most illnesses.

- Diabetics have inflammation issues.

- Eat anti-inflammatory foods that are high in antioxidants.

- Stress causes inflammation.

- Poor digestive systems contribute to inflammation.

- Sugar is an inflammatory food.

- Use raw kale or spinach in smoothies to fight inflammation.

- Fatty acids and Omega 3s are anti-inflammatory foods.

Exercise your right

Exercise your right to happiness, health and the best life you could possibly have with, you guessed it, exercise. Chronic stress seems to be taking over our lives and, left unmanaged, it will bring forth serious health consequences. Stress causes muscle tension and high blood pressure due to the excess adrenaline pumping through our bodies with no outlet. Moderate regular physical activity provides this much needed release. There is no substitute for exercise and the best exercise is to move your body to a point where your heartbeat rises. Our bodies were created to move and have a great need to move. Today, due to our sedentary lifestyles and ongoing stress, our bodies are under-worked and it is affecting not only our physical health but mental health as well. Imagine how a border collie would feel not being able to move day after day. It would be very unhappy and eventually become depressed.

With antidepressant prescriptions skyrocketing, depression is becoming a mental health epidemic in North America. In experimental studies exercise is used as a treatment for depression. Exercise is becoming recognized for its psychological benefits as much as its physical ones as Dr. Smits and Dr. Otto have stated in an article in Time Magazine in June, 2010: "Exercise appears to affect, like an antidepressant, particular neurotransmitter systems in the brain, and it helps patients with depression re-establish positive behaviors." Mental health specialists are not the only ones realizing the benefits of exercise in treating stress, anxiety and depression. Cesar Millan, the Dog Whisperer, also uses a treadmill for treating dogs with anxiety. Moving the body seems to have a psychological as well as a physiological effect and it brings on a tranquilizing state.

The body releases chemicals called endorphins that are as potent as morphine. Endorphins bring on positive moods and boost self-esteem. Exercise also provides an outlet for negative moods such as stress, anger or frustration. Therefore exercise can lift positive feelings and quell negative feelings. When you have a low mood it may be difficult to motivate yourself to get up and start exercising. Giving yourself small goals each day such as a ten-minute walk will start the momentum towards increasing your physical activity. As each day passes, with exercise as part of your daily activity, your energy and coping skills will increase and your moods will get a boost pushing you forward to a happier and healthier life.

Sweet dreams, sweet life

We may feel that sleeping takes our precious time away from doing the important tasks we feel we need to do. But our lives depend on a good night's rest. Have you ever had three consecutive nights of little or no sleep? You probably felt like an accident waiting to happen. Our bodies depend on our shutting down for a little shut-eye in order to replenish and restore our batteries. Prior to 1930 people were getting an average of nine hours or more of sleep. Since 1970 we have been averaging less than seven hours of sleep. That trend is building up a big sleep deficit and making our society a little more irritable and less tolerant. **Here are some benefits we experience from eight to nine hours of sleep:**

Healthy heart

Your heart pumps hundreds of gallons of blood each day which takes about 100,000 beats. If you are stressed or feeling under pressure your blood pressure rises, which makes your heart work harder. This amazing muscle needs a break and will be healthier if you get eight hours' sleep. Sleep apnea causes much strain on the heart and puts sufferers at a greater risk of heart attack.

May prevent cancer

Melatonin, a hormone secreted by the pinal gland in the brain, has been linked to suppressing the growth of tumors. Melatonin is produced while we sleep. Any light exposure, even from a bright alarm clock, can disrupt the melatonin process. Be sure to sleep in a dark room. The best time for melatonin production is between one a.m. and three a.m.

Reduces stress

Today our bodies are under attack and on high alert with chronic stress and multitasking. This not only takes a toll on our cortisol hormone but also raises our blood pressure. "As little as one hour of lost sleep can increase cortisol levels by 50 percent and interfere with insulin function." *(The Cortisol Connection Diet, Shawn Talbott, PH.D.)* This increases your risk of heart attacks and strokes. Also melatonin (relaxing hormone) and serotonin (happy hormone) levels are replenished during adequate sleep.

Makes you more alert

When you wake up feeling refreshed you have more energy. Having more energy increases your need to be active which results in other health benefits and a good chance for another good night's rest.

Boosts your memory and mental health

Researchers are coming to understand that during sleep your body is resting and the brain is processing your day's events making connections between feelings and memories. Proper sleep enables us to remember and better process things including new skills we have learned that day. Good sleepers are better performers. Chronic sleep deprivation will result in poor mental health. Racing thoughts, obsessive thinking and low moods are a few symptoms of a large sleep deficit. Dr. Dan Robotham, senior researcher at the Mental Health Foundation, believes that people can get stuck in a spiral where poor sleep leads to mental health problems, which lead to worse sleep. *(BBC News Health, January 26, 2011)*

Helps your body repair and replenish

During the day our bodies' cells are being damaged by stress, ultra-violet rays, toxins and other harmful exposures. In the second phase of sleep called Slow Wave Sleep, all our systems start a healing process where cells are being replaced or repaired. This process takes two hours and is essential for the survival of the body and mind.

Sleep controls appetite the next day

The hormone, leptin, is important in giving us the feeling of satisfaction after eating. Low levels of leptin tell the body there is a shortage of food even after we have finished eating. Leptin levels are replenished after a good night's sleep, helping us suppress our appetites. The hormone, ghrelin, is our hungry hormone. After a short night's sleep, ghrelin levels are elevated, making us feel hungry all the time. Decreased leptin levels tell the body there is a calorie shortage and promote "false" hunger by ghrelin. The balance of leptin and ghrelin is significant in controlling appetite and maintaining healthy weight.

Not a good sleeper?

There are many variables that get in the way of a good sleep such as too much caffeine, stress or stimulation before bedtime. Try shutting off all electronics, including your cell phone and relaxing in a dimly lit room 30 minutes before bedtime. Melatonin can be used to regulate sleep patterns. It's a safer alternative to over-the-counter or prescription sleeping pills. Melatonin is not for prolonged use but can be helpful in starting a healthy sleep pattern. It also has antioxidant benefits as it can inhibit oxidative damage and provide some anti-aging benefits. It's found in most drug stores and health food stores.

Not everyone needs eight hours of sleep to feel fresh and alert. But everyone needs a good restful environment to get continuous, uninterrupted sleep. The bedroom should not have a TV or computer. They keep us stimulated, not allowing time for us to feel relaxed and sleepy. The bed and bedding should be comfortable. Don't cheap out on a mattress or pillows. We spend a lot of time in our lives sleeping. Going to bed twenty minutes before your usual bedtime gives you some quiet thinking time to go over the day's events or tomorrow's tasks. Many people find it difficult to fall asleep because the brain is demanding attention on some important details. Write these things down to settle your inner voice. A cool, dark room is the best environment for sleeping through the night. Some people enjoy a soft fan blowing on them for extra comfort. Your body temperature needs to cool down in order for a deep sleep to occur and the repairing and healing to begin.

If you suffer from chronic sleep disruptions or insomnia, it is important to consult your doctor as these can result in major health issues if not addressed.

Strength in numbers

Sometimes our health and weight loss goals tend to slip away as we each start feeling we are the only one who seems to care. Peer pressure from partners, kids, and co-workers who don't appreciate your straying from the norm can also sabotage your plans. The good thing is that there are people out there who share your goals and it's time to seek them out. Check out your Facebook or Twitter contact page and start gathering a few people from your network to form a wellness support group. Here are some tips to get you started:

Gather people who can commit to a full three months. It will take that much time for some changes to become comfortable and part of your daily life. Try to keep the group small at first in order to organize meetings, email lists and special activities.

- Facebook and Twitter are amazing resources to keep connected any time of the day.

- Set a date every week (even if not everyone can make it) to meet for tea or lunch. Try out new places together that offer healthy choices. Many restaurants have their menus online. Decide on another weekly mini-goal and discuss the prior week's challenges and triumphs of putting it into action.

- It is very important not to discuss pounds for the first six weeks, even if you are excited to do so. Everyone's body is different therefore everyone loses weight at a different rate. Some may become discouraged if they haven't dropped a pound. Keep your focus on wellness and support at the beginning as adjusting to your new eating style is going to require some love and tenderness.

- Plan activities a couple of times a month such as a movie night, bowling, golfing or checking out a new Zumba class. If your partner is pouting because you are having so much fun, then invite your partner (notify the group) as long as he/she respects the goals of the group.

- Have a monthly potluck when all members bring a new and exciting dish they have discovered. Be sure to bring the recipe and place where ingredients can be found.

- Notify each other through email or texting when you find an item on sale at the grocery store. Eating healthier will cost more than eating junky; this also can deter people from sticking to the plan.

- Always stick to your weekly meetings even if two or three people can't make it. Those who can't make the meeting should follow up with the next mini-goal and any future plans. We are fortunate to be connected through technology so use it to your advantage.

- Give your club a name. It gives the feeling of unity and empowerment. Once the word gets around and others see you looking great and having fun, people will want to join your "club."

Support plays a large role in any situation where change is needed. There are many groups that have become successful and well known such as AA and Weight Watchers. Remember these groups started with just a few people. Drawing on your resources is better than going on alone. One can be a lonely number when trying to move forward in a progressive manner, plus it's more fun when you have all your buddies surrounding you!

CHAPTER 2

FEED YOUR MOODS, CHANGE YOUR BODY

"If ignorance were bliss, there would be more happy people."

Victor Cousins

It's all fun and games until mortality taps us on the shoulder. Now that we have an understanding of the importance of nourishment for our bodies and minds, let us put it into action.

Your first month, your first thoughts

Your brain is a very powerful entity controlling every part of you, voluntarily and involuntarily. If you have negative thoughts or a negative self-image, you will need to be aware of how they may be getting in the way of your goals.

Instead of focusing on losing weight (*or why you're not losing weight*) focus on nurturing and replenishing your body with the vital nutrients needed to decrease the effects of aging and increase youthfulness and energy. By making this mental switch you aren't counting calories, feeling guilty and giving up on healthy eating.

My three easiest tips to remember are:

1. **If it doesn't grow, it isn't good for you.**
2. **If it rots, it's good for you.**
3. **If it doesn't nourish your body, it isn't good for you.**

It's not the calories that are your biggest worry; it's the havoc that bad foods will create inside you. Many people are drawn to the "low-calorie" or "only 100 calories" labels on packaging. You are better off eating 200 calories of almonds than 100 calories of over-processed snacks.

Your goals, in addition to weight loss, should be to cleanse, rebuild, revive, heal, rebalance and re-establish your physical and mental well-being. The withdrawals for the first month will be rough and ugly as you are cleaning out all the lingering toxins that have made their home in your cells for years. Your body and mind have become addicted to the actual foods that are making you sick and lethargic. The elimination process is a difficult period because your body is breaking down all the toxins and gunk, layer by layer. Toxins come out many ways including through your pores. Your body is basically coughing and gagging out all the garbage through every orifice available. This also takes a lot of energy so be aware that you may need a nap every now and then.

Super Size Me filmmaker Morgan Spurlock detoxified himself using a raw-only diet for eight weeks and had major withdrawals for the first two weeks including headaches, sweating and the shakes. He states it was like coming off of a drug addiction as he was addicted to the foods and additives that were making him sick. Slowly weaning from sugars or sweeteners may be an easier process for some people; however you will need to be cutting back more and more every week.

When you start incorporating more raw vegetables and fruits and less sugar, salt and trans-fats in your diet, your entire make-up and physical being are being upgraded and shifting to a healthier and higher level. You may need to start small by cutting out only deep-fried, fatty foods. Then next month try eliminating sugars and sweeteners and so on.

Give yourself six months to a year to get there. Eventually you will get the energy and results you are looking for and you will want to maintain them at all costs. Focus on the goal of rejuvenation and healing. Reprogram and shift your thinking about food and your behavior will match your thoughts. Thoughts become things.

Lifestyle/food journal

It is important to chart for the first seven days to assess whether you are finding any problem areas or challenges. This is for your benefit and eyes only unless you choose to share and require support.

Day 1

Breakfast

Snack

Lunch

Snack

Supper

Beverages

Other

Exercise _____ for _____ minutes

Day 2

Breakfast

Snack

Lunch

Snack

Supper

Beverages

Other

Exercise _____ for _____ minutes

Day 3

Breakfast

Snack

Lunch

Snack

Supper

Beverages

Other

Exercise   for   minutes

Day 4

Breakfast

Snack

Lunch

Snack

Supper

Beverages

Other

Exercise   for   minutes

After 4 days how are you feeling? You are halfway there.

_____

_____

_____

_____

_____

_____

_____

_____

Day 5

Breakfast

Snack

Lunch

Snack

Supper

Beverages

Other

Exercise   for   minutes

Day 6

Breakfast _____

Snack _____

Lunch _____

Snack _____

Supper _____

Beverages _____

Other _____

Exercise _____ for _____ minutes

Day 7

Breakfast _____

Snack _____

Lunch _____

Snack _____

Supper _____

Beverages _____

Other _____

Exercise _____ for _____ minutes

Congratulations! You made 7 days of trying to make improvements in your health. Make notes of any pitfalls and your low mood periods; also what seemed to work and where you could tune things up.

Pitfalls

Low mood periods

What seemed to work

Improvement needed

Breakfast Options
Tip: Pick a high protein breakfast to sustain energy and stamina.

- Cooked oatmeal with cinnamon, chia seed and almond milk
- Plain Greek yogurt with fruit and flax oil
- Toasted whole-wheat English muffin and almond butter
- 2 eggs and 1 slice of sprouted grains toast
- 1 egg on toasted whole wheat English muffin
- 2 cups of cereal (under 6 gr. of sugar) add almonds and All Bran
- Sonny Boy cereal with cinnamon and hemp hearts
- Handful of nuts and a protein smoothie

10 a.m. Snack Options
- Small can of flavored tuna with Melba toast or brown rice crackers
- Handful of almonds with a piece of fruit
- **2 cups of raw veggies**
- 3/4 cup cottage cheese with fruit
- Melba toast (4 pieces) and almond butter
- Smoothie with avocado
- 1 boiled egg with Melba toast

Trick is if you didn't eat protein for breakfast, pick a protein for the snack. Remember to drink two cups of green or white tea during the day. Smoothies made with fresh berries, blended Greek yogurt, avocado, cold green tea with POM juice and fruit make good snacks or desserts.

Try to eat five times a day in order to keep sugar and insulin levels stable. Eating regularly will make your body burn calories, plus keep your blood sugar stable and your brain alert. Keep snacks on hand whether in your car, purse or office drawer. Invest in an insulated lunch bag. **Also eating a raw food at every meal helps with digestion, transportation, and absorption of nutrients. Green salads make perfect side dishes.**

Lunch

Tip: Best to eat about two hours after the last time you ate.

- Salad with added protein (tuna, chicken, beans, chickpeas or nuts) for satisfaction. Olive oil & balsamic dressing are best.
- **2 cups of raw veggies** and can of tuna, sardines or salmon with pepper and lemon juice.
- 2 boiled eggs on English muffin or toasted rye bread.
- 1 cup of chili with a side of pumpernickel bread (and pat of butter).
- Veggie, chicken or bean wrap with light dressing.
- Any kind of homemade soup. Add lentils or beans for more fiber.
- Turkey or chicken sandwich on whole grain bread or in a wrap. Add some raw veggies such as shredded carrots or sprouts.

3:00 Snack

Tip: See last snack options.

If you haven't eaten **2 cups of raw veggies** you need to, before supper. Need sugar or carbs? Try these:
- Frozen bananas dipped in melted dark chocolate;
- Pita chips and hummus or guacamole;
- Apples or pineapple with stevia and cinnamon;
- Tortillas and salsa;
- Starbucks chia lattes with 1/2 vanilla flavoring or none;
- 2 digestive cookies or low sugar cookies (under 4 g);
- 2 squares of dark chocolate.

Supper

Tip: Always serve on a small plate and have a side salad. Have some carbs to raise serotonin levels such as potatoes, sweet potatoes, brown rice, turnip or squash.

- Big bowl of soup (low sodium) with a tomato and cucumber sandwich.
- Bowl of chili (vegetarian with lots of beans is the best option) with toasted rye bread and small salad.
- Any piece of meat or fish with sides of brown rice or potatoes and veggies or salad.
- Pita sandwich with tuna, chicken or egg with veggies and bowl of soup.
- Grilled salmon (with dill), small potato and salad.
- Chicken wrapped in whole wheat wrap with salad makings.
- Extra-lean hamburger on toasted whole wheat English muffin with salad.
- Left-over chili mixed with rice in whole wheat wrap with low fat cheese.
- Shrimp stir-fry with brown rice noodles.
- Spinach and feta omelet in whole wheat wrap.

To maximize benefits put cooked quinoa or barley with brown rice and eat more beans and lentils than meat. For chili, add extra beans/lentils for maximum benefits.

See recipe for chili on page 152.

Dessert

- 2 low sugar cookies (under 5 grams of sugar ex. Digestive cookies);
- Yogurt smoothie; Any fruit with real whipping cream;
- Home-made baking with whole wheat or spelt flour.

See recipe for baking items on pages 141 and 142 and frozen bananas on page 146.

Important Parts of the Plan

- Eat a handful of nuts twice a day.
- Drink lots of water throughout the day.
- Drink 2 cups of green tea/white tea a day.
- Eat 2–3 cups of raw veggies a day or at every meal.
- Limit red meat to once or twice a week.
- Eat fish at least twice a week.
- Lentils and beans in your meals are perfect for weight loss.
- No white flour, white sugar, white rice, white pasta.
- No pop and limit fruit juices.
- No skipping meals or snacks.
- Breakfast is a must.
- 25–30 grams minimum of fiber a day.
- Incorporate good fats in meals or snacks.

10 day detox

A detox is not for weight loss but for cleansing the body.

Dairy products: yogurt, cheese, milk, cream, and sour cream. Only goat cheese and feta cheese are allowed.

All grains that contain gluten: If the package doesn't state gluten-free it is not allowed. Oatmeal is gluten-free but is not allowed. Rices are allowed.

Corn: Anything that has corn or corn by-products

Oils: Only olive oil, almond oil and coconut oil are allowed.

Alcohol and caffeine: Herbal teas and green tea are allowed.

Peanuts and products containing peanuts: no peanut butter.

Sugar: Any ingredient in foods that ends with "ose" is pretty much sugar. No table sugar, brown sugar or artificial sweeteners. Stevia can be used.

Citrus fruit: only lemons are allowed.

Meats: only turkey, chicken and wild salmon are allowed after seven days.

Seafood: No shelled seafood or tuna.

- **For protein use eggs, beans, quinoa, lentils, fish, almonds, almond butter and pistachios.**
- **For milks, use almond or rice milk.**
- **No soy products during this stage.**

Please EAT!

- Unlimited vegetables. Be sure to eat at least two cups of raw vegetables a day. Cooked vegetables lose 50 to 80 percent of their valuable nutrients (except tomatoes). The more raw vegetables you eat the better.

- Stir-fried veggies are also a good way to cook if you only cook until they are transparent and softer, not browned. Omelets are an easy way to get your protein and veggies; be creative! For salads, throw in some tuna, chicken, avocado or seeds.

- Homemade soup or vegetarian chili is also a satisfying meal. Find a gluten-free bread and dip in olive oil for side.

- Fill up on fruit (except citrus fruits); an excellent form is a fruit salad for dessert. A smoothie can be made with almond, hemp or rice milk. Ripe mangos make a frothy smoothie.

- Bean and gluten-free grain salads are tasty. Lentils are a super power food to add to soups, chilis or wherever.

Complement Your Success with....

- a natural digestive enzyme for ten days;
- drinking eight to ten glasses of water a day;
- taking supplements such as flax oil & 5-HTP;
- eating nuts and a non-citrus fruit in between meals;
- sleeping seven to eight hours a night;
- sweating through exercise or sauna.

Optional but Effective: Drink filtered water with one tsp. of apple cider vinegar or real squeezed lemon juice.

After Detox try using as a snack: Mix one tbsp. of organic flax oil (needs to be refrigerated) with cottage cheese. May need to add fruit or nuts for taste. Needs to be mixed well so oil does not float to top. If you have flaxseeds, grind and immediately use.

Mango Smoothie

1 cup	coconut milk
1	ripe mango
7–8	leaves of spinach
3–4	ice cubes

This smoothie is excellent if you are craving something sweet.

After 10 days . . .

If possible try reintroducing one food every couple of days in order to identify any side effects or negative symptoms. An example would be to start introducing gluten foods first to recognize any discomfort, bloating, allergic reaction or low energy and moods. This is helpful in pinning down foods that your body cannot tolerate.

Stock your shelves

Spinach leaves
Whole-wheat flour
Quinoa
Green tea
Frozen blueberries
Brown rice
Ground flax meal
Ground chia seed
Popcorn kernels
Bananas
Wild salmon
Chicken breasts
Whole-wheat wraps
Salsa

Cranberries
Yogurt
Butter
Olive oil
Eggs
Beans (*red and black*)
English muffins (*whole wheat*)
Almonds and walnuts
Potatoes / Sweet potatoes
Bell peppers (*red and orange*)
Almond butter
Frozen vegetables
Organic cereal (*under 5g of sugar*)

Having these items on hand at all times ensures that you will have many healthy menu varieties at all meal and snack times.

Examples:
- Spinach salad with cranberries,
- Bell pepper and nuts
- Egg on toasted English muffin
- Yogurt smoothie with banana, chia and blueberries
- Cereal with cranberries and nuts
- Chicken breast cooked in olive oil with brown rice and veggies
- Chicken wrap with salsa, beans and rice
- Tuna wrap with spinach leaves and bell peppers

Tips: Use whole-wheat flour, ground flax meal and chia in baking.
Mix quinoa with brown rice for protein.

"My hope is different: that people will acknowledge the declining of both our soil and nutrient content of our foods and do something to repair those losses—not merely do further studies!"

Carolyn Dean, MD, ND
The Magnesium Miracle, 2007

Super foods on a budget

- eggs (*farm eggs better*)
- organic plain yogurt or Greek yogurt
- raw seeds and nuts (*unsalted*)
- frozen blueberries and strawberries
- barley
- green tea
- spinach or kale
- garlic
- wild rice
- lentils
- almond milk
- oatmeal

Super foods in health stores

- quinoa
- coconut oil (*organic, virgin*)
- cacao powder
- spirulina (*can also be in supplement form*)
- hemp hearts or seeds
- organic coffee
- Stevia—natural sweetener has no effect on blood sugar
- goji berries
- buckwheat
- ground chia seed or salba
- organic ground flax meal or flax oil
- kefir

More *Food4Thought* **tidbits**

- According to long-standing research in China, celery lowers blood pressure. So do bananas.

- Two tbsp. of ketchup have two tsp. of sugar; BBQ sauce has three.

- If you aren't an elite athlete, stay away from sports drinks.

- Cinnamon is an amazing antioxidant and lowers blood sugar.

- Walnuts and almonds can be thrown into salads and cereals.

- Start baking with whole-wheat flour and Stevia.

- Don't eat any charred, barbeque meat; it's very toxic.

- Check out your nearest health food store; it's not just for health junkies; it has really cool stuff!

- If you need to be energized, smell a citrus fruit; then eat it!

- Butter is better than hard-block margarine and shortening.

- If you are supplementing vitamin D consider the vitamin D-K2 combination.

- Dark chocolate contains the much-needed nutrient magnesium. Buy high quality low-sugar chocolate. A little nibble goes further than cheap chocolate bars.

- Watch sugar content of flavored yogurts. You're better off getting plain and throwing in fruit.

- Washing fruit and putting it in a bowl on the kitchen counter will increase everyone's chances of eating more fruit.

- For quick salad, buy packaged leaves and a bag of trail mix with cranberries. Cut up red or yellow pepper. Mix.

- Buy 5 lb. weights and set them beside the couch. You can do curls while watching TV. It's that easy to get moving.

- Don't ever buy prepackaged baked goods, seriously!

- MSG should be avoided at all costs. It raises insulin levels and lowers blood sugar. This is why you are hungry an hour later when eating oriental food with MSG. Bad stuff!

- All oils and butter can turn into a trans fat if heated too high. If it's smoking, it's now a trans fat.

- Coconuts, coconut milk and unrefined coconut oil are good fats.

- The sun is healing; take in some sunshine twenty minutes a day.

- People are breathing too shallowly, which results in low oxygen levels. Take five minutes a day to take deep breaths. The results are amazing!

- Fruit juice is made from low-grade fruit. It is also highly heated during processing, killing all digestive enzymes. Eat fruit.

- Magnesium has three hundred essential functions in the body. One is to relax you. Increased sugar and processed foods lower magnesium levels.

- Gluten in wheat gives foods their "puff" but they are very hard on our digestive system. Think of water mixed with flour: paste!

- We need nutrients more than ever as our stress hormones are being depleted. Eat foods with essential amino acids.

- Teas are helpful in de-stressing. Try a chai tea, delicious!

- Cellulose is a chemically processed wood pulp that is added to many diet foods to add bulk without adding calories.

- Cellulose cannot be efficiently digested by humans.

- Cellulose is also used in wallpaper paste and insulation.

- A popular additive called L-Cysteine, is used to enhance bread and baked goods is commonly made from feathers and human hair.

- Sweeteners do not provide the energy sugar does which causes the body to increase hunger in order to make up for the absence of calories.

- What we call weeds in our gardens was once used as traditional medicine. Learn about what is growing in your yard.

- Add chopped parsley in soups, stews, sauces, egg dishes and mashed potatoes for extra antioxidants.

- To get all the nutritional benefits from grains, soak for a couple of hours first. This is also easier on the digestive system.

- Sesame seeds contribute to good mental health as they contain L-tryptophan.

- Choose tea over coffee as much as you can; however organic coffee is higher in antioxidants than conventional coffee.

- Try tuna, salmon or sardines with dill and lemon juice as a snack or throw in a wrap.

CHAPTER 3

RECIPES FOR LIFE

"You don't have to cook fancy or
complicated masterpieces—just
good food from fresh ingredients."

Julia Child

Shortcuts to healthy eating

Always have packaged spinach or spring mix leaves on hand. Here are some examples of quick salads:

- add sliced boiled eggs and mushrooms

- add tuna, salmon or cut up chicken and veggies

- add red onion, yellow pepper and cranberry trail mix

- add quartered mandarin oranges, red onion and pecans

- add warm beets, cranberries, goat cheese and walnuts

- add diced tomatoes, red onion, basil and green pepper mixed in olive oil with dried oregano; add a little feta on top

- add some chopped pickles, celery, chives and tuna

For a healthy dressing try mixing orange juice, red wine vinegar and olive oil.

- Use leftover chili in wraps or pitas with brown rice and a little cheddar cheese. Kids love them! Or for a soup, add more water and some chopped jalapeños.

- When making a pot of brown rice, add wild rice and quinoa. Make a big pot to use in three to four meals. For one meal, add a seven-grain salad from the deli and mix.

- Lots of grocery stores have cut up veggies ready for stir-fry. Saves money in the long run as it prevents unused veggies from spoiling. Throw in with cubed cooked meat to soften. Add a little low-sodium oyster sauce and lots of rice noodles. A meal in 15 minutes.

- Buy chicken breasts in bulk, wrap individually and put in freezer. These defrost easier and can make a chicken salad or chicken wrap in 10 minutes.

- Always have lots of varieties of veggies in the freezer. Excellent choices are broccoli, peas and oriental mix.

- Serve more than scrambled eggs. Cook with tomatoes, basil, parsley, spinach and onions. Put in a whole-wheat wrap with salsa and cheese. Yummy!

- Buy prepackaged coleslaw mix and fry in olive oil with pepper.

- Remember to add spices for powerful antioxidant benefits.

Banana Berry Muffins

1 cup	whole-wheat flour
1/4 cup	ground flax
1/2 cup	rolled oats
1/4 tsp	cinnamon
1/3 cup	sugar (*or 2 tsp of Stevia*)
2 tsp	baking powder
2	medium mashed bananas
1/4 cup	cup canola oil
1	beaten egg (*Omega-3 best*)
2/3 cup	of almond milk
1/2 cup	cup raspberries, blueberries or dried cranberries
1/4 cup	cup walnuts (*optional*)

Mix all dry ingredients in a large bowl. Make a well in the middle and add banana, oil, egg and milk. Mix thoroughly and then add berries and walnuts. Put in a little more milk if you feel it's needed. Keep fairly thick. Spoon in muffin cups and put in preheated oven of 350 degrees. Bake until golden brown or toothpick comes out clean.

Date Cookies

8	Medium sized dates
1	banana
1 1/2 cups	unrefined coconut flakes

Remove pits from dates. Place all ingredients in blender and process until smooth. Add more coconut if not thick enough. Bake at 325 for 10–15 minutes or until done and golden brown. Cookies will be soft but will hold together. Taste sweet but very healthy!

Coconut Almond Butter Balls

1 cup	almond butter
1/2 cup	honey
1/4 cup	coconut oil
3/4 cup	cocoa or cacao powder
1 cup	shredded coconut
1/2 cup	chopped pecans or walnuts
1/2 tsp	cinnamon

Mix all ingredients together. Put in fridge for 20 minutes until batter gets harder. Roll balls in shredded coconut. Freeze balls until desired hardness.

Better-For-You Chocolate Chip Cookies

2 cups	whole-wheat flour	1/2 cup	packed brown sugar
2	eggs	1 tsp	Stevia (*powder*)
1/4 cup	ground flax meal	1 tbsp	vanilla
1/2 tsp	baking powder	1/2 pkg	chocolate chips (*dark*)
1/2 tsp	baking soda	1/2 cup	walnuts (*optional*)
1/2 tsp	cinnamon	1/4 cup	cranberries
1	cup butter		

Preheat oven to 350 degrees. Combine flour and dry ingredients in small bowl. In large bowl, beat butter and sugar. Then add eggs and vanilla until smooth. Gradually beat flour mixture into butter mixture until all combined. If it does not seem thick enough add another cup flour. Stir in chocolate chips (and walnuts and cranberries). Bake until golden brown.

Cabbage Coleslaw

1 pkg	bagged cabbage with shredded carrot
1/2 cup	peeled and shredded white onion
1/2 cup	orange, red or yellow (*or all* 3) peppers, chopped

Dressing:

1/3 cup	plain yogurt
1/2 tbsp	lemon juice
1/2 tbsp	vinegar
1 tsp	mustard
1/2 tsp	caraway seed
1/4 tsp	Stevia

Mix dressing ingredients and stir in with cabbage/vegetables.

Fried Cabbage

1 pkg	bagged cabbage with shredded carrot	1 tsp	olive oil
		1/2 tsp	freshly ground pepper
1/2 tsp	butter		

Heat butter and oil in pan and throw in whole package of cabbage. May overflow but eventually cabbage will soften and fit in pan. Do not brown but soften cabbage. Pepper before serving. Makes an excellent side dish. Next time try adding fresh sliced white mushrooms and chopped onion.

Left over fried cabbage? Make a quick soup by adding organic vegetable broth. Throw in corn, chives and stewed tomatoes. Heat and serve. Make cabbage rolls with ground turkey and brown rice. Top with organic tomato sauce. Vibrant colored cabbage contains premium nutrients.

Dill Dressing

1/4 cup	cup extra virgin olive oil
3 tbsp	lemon juice (*freshly squeezed best*)
1 1/2 tbsp	chopped fresh or dried dill
1/2 tsp	salt
1/2 tsp	fresh ground pepper

Greek Dressing

1/4 cup	olive oil
1/4 cup	red wine vinegar
2 heaping tbsp	crumbled feta cheese
1/2 tsp	minced garlic
Freshly chopped oregano (or dried)	

Bruschetta

6–7	Tomatoes (*Roma best*)	1 tbsp	balsamic vinegar
		1/4 cup	yellow onion, chopped
2 cloves	garlic minced	6	fresh basil leaves, chopped
2 tbsp	extra virgin olive oil	Freshly ground pepper to taste	

Skinned tomatoes work best, however, not mandatory. To skin tomatoes boil in hot water for 5 minutes then submerse in cold water. Skins should come off easily. Cut tomatoes in quarters and remove seeds and stems. Chop finely and put in bowl. Mix all ingredients.

Sugar-Free Mochaccino

Cup of very hot brewed coffee
2 tsp   coconut milk
1/4 cup   unsweetened chocolate almond milk
1/2 pkg   Stevia (*or tsp*)
Sprinkle of cinnamon and nutmeg

Tomato Basil Eggs

3 Farm eggs
Milk
One small chopped tomato
Chopped onion (*desired amount*)
6 spinach leaves
Basil

Melt butter in pan and stir-fry tomato, onion and spinach until spinach is wilted. Whisk eggs in a little bit of milk and pour in pan. Add basil. If you have feta cheese kicking around, throw some in as well and roll in a wrap.

Veggie Stir-Fry

Mushrooms (*sliced*)
Water chestnuts (*sliced*)
Onion (*chopped*)
Celery (*chopped*)
Shredded carrots
Snap peas

Bean sprouts
Broccoli florets
Rice noodles
Low sodium, low sugar
(*under 4 grams*) Asian sauce

Stir-fry veggies in olive oil until transparent. Add sauce. Cook noodles according to directions and mix together.

Frozen Bananas

Take a peeled banana and split in half.
Melt 1/2 tsp butter or virgin coconut oil and 1 cup of dark chocolate chips and stir together. Spread or pour over banana. Sprinkle crushed walnuts on chocolate. Freeze.

If you have left over melted chocolate roll in some prunes and freeze. Perfect for that sweet craving and kids love them!

Craving salt? Try celery sticks or pita chips with hummus or guacamole. Kick-start metabolism by putting cayenne pepper on your hummus!

Homemade Apple Crisp

8	organic apples (*peeled and sliced*)
1/2 cup	cup chopped rhubarb (*optional*)
1 tsp	cinnamon
1/2 cup	soft butter
1/4 cup	brown sugar or 4 pkgs Stevia (*4 tsp*)
1 tsp	nutmeg
2 tsp	alba/ground chia seed
1 tsp	hemp seed
1 cup	oatmeal (*large flakes*)
1/4 cup	walnut pieces
1 cup	whole-wheat flour

In a square glass baking dish arrange peeled apple pieces. Sprinkle tsp of cinnamon. You can add cup of chopped rhubarb but will need to sprinkle 1 pkg (1 tsp) of Stevia over apples and rhubarb. If not using rhubarb then don't use Stevia. In a medium sized bowl, take soft butter and add sugar or Stevia and all dry ingredients (plus walnuts) and mix with hands. Should make a crumbly mix. Take crumbly mixture and put on top of apples and press. Bake at 350 degrees for 50 minutes.

Tip: You can replace 1/2 of the butter with coconut oil.

Mandarin Spinach Salad

1	bunch spinach leaves (*washed*)
4	mandarin oranges
1	quarter red onion thinly sliced
1/2 cup	goat, feta or blue cheese
1/2 cup	slivered almonds or walnuts
1 cup	white chicken breast (*optional*)

Dressing:

6 tbsp	olive oil
5 tbsp	orange juice (*freshly squeezed best*)
4 tbsp	red wine vinegar

Servings: 4 (side dish)

Cucumber Celery Salad

1	large cucumber, thinly sliced
2	large celery stalks, chopped
2 cups	iceberg lettuce, chopped
1	small apple, thinly sliced
1/2 cup	walnuts
1/4 cup	cranberries (*optional*)

Dressing:

1/2 cup	plain yogurt
3 tbsp	vinegar
1/2 pkg	Stevia (*1/2 tsp*)

Dash of organic sea salt and pepper

Servings: 4 (side dish)

Orange Nut Bread

1 cup	whole-wheat flour
1/3 cup	ground flax or wheat germ
6 packages	Stevia (6 *tsp*)
1 tbsp	orange zest
1 cup	apple butter
1/4 cup	canola oil
1	whole egg
1/4 cup	milk or almond milk
2 tsp	vanilla
1/2 cup	dried cranberries (optional)
1/4 cup	walnut crumbs
1 tsp	cinnamon or pumpkin pie spice

In large bowl, blend dry ingredients and dried cranberries and walnuts. Add egg, vanilla, oil, milk, apple butter, and zest. Blend with wooden spoon. Grease pan with butter and pour batter in loaf pan. Bake at 350 degrees for 45 minutes.

Powerhouse Salad

Everything you need in a delicious salad!

Spring-mixed leaves
Spinach leaves
Bean sprouts
Chopped red or yellow bell pepper
Shaved carrot
Pumpkin seeds

Chopped avocado
Chopped red onion
Sliced cucumbers
Pomegranate seeds
Sliced cucumbers

Make in large salad bowl. Make it a meal and add a cut up chicken breast. Use a vinaigrette dressing.

Bean Wrap

1 can of rinsed black beans
1 can of rinsed chickpeas
Chopped green onion
Chopped tomato
Salsa

Chopped romaine lettuce
Chopped green or red pepper
Plain yogurt
Chopped fresh cilantro
Chopped jalapeño pepper

Mash beans and peas slightly. Put on stone-ground or whole-wheat wrap with other ingredients and a dollop of yogurt and salsa.

Protein Packed Meatloaf

Kids will definitely be open and willing to eat this! If they want to throw some ketchup on it, no worries; they are getting a lot of good stuff without even knowing it!

1 pound	lean ground beef	1/4 tsp	minced garlic
1/2 pound	ground turkey	1/4 tsp	paprika
1/2 cup	cooked quinoa	1 tsp	ground chia seed
1 large farm	egg (*or regular egg*)	1/4 cup	chopped onions
3/4 cup	canned or cooked lentils	1/4 cup	oatmeal
1/4 cup	salsa	3/4 cup	grated zucchini (*optional*)

Mix all ingredients in a really large bowl. Pat in a loaf pan and put a little tomato sauce on top for flavor. Cook for 75 minutes at 350 degrees. I usually like to make this the night before or on a Sunday afternoon.

Tip: Wrap potatoes or sweet potatoes in foil and stick in oven while meatloaf is cooking. Serve with potatoes and salad.

My husband likes his meatloaf sliced on toasted multi-grain bread with a slice of cheddar cheese for his lunch the next day!

Protein Galore Chili

1 cup	quinoa
1 can	organic diced tomatoes
1 can	red kidney beans
1 can	black kidney beans
1 can	lentils
1 cup	salsa (*desired heat*)
1 small can	tomato paste
1/4 cup	water
1 pkg	ground turkey (*or lean ground beef*)
2 tbsp	dried chives or 1/3 cup of chopped chives
2 tbsp	chili powder
Chopped cilantro	

Cook quinoa by 1 part grain and 2 parts water. Pour tomatoes in bowl; stir in olive oil. Brown ground meat in a separate pot or deep pan. Drain any grease. Pour tomatoes and oil in with ground meat and mix. Put in tomato paste and water. Stir in kidney beans, lentils and salsa. Cook throughout for 8–10 minutes. Before serving, stir in quinoa and cilantro.

Approximate cooking time 30 minutes. Serves 4–5 people.

Roasted Vegetables

1	zucchini halved and sliced thick
1	yellow squash halved and sliced thick
1 large	sweet potato peeled and chopped in chunks
5	red potatoes peeled and chopped in chunks
1/2	yellow or red onion chopped
1	clove of garlic chopped

Put chopped vegetables on 3 or 4 pieces of aluminum foil and drizzle with olive oil. Sprinkle basil, and other desired spices. Wrap and set on heated barbeque for 30 minutes or until potatoes are tender.

Quick Veggie Fettuccine

1 small pkg	cherry tomatoes (*halved*)
1 small	zucchini
1 small	yellow squash
1/4 cup	grated Parmesan
1 package	whole-wheat pasta
1/4 cup	olive oil

2 tsp	tomato pesto
2 tsp	Dijon mustard
Pepper	
Fresh or dried basil	
Handful chopped chives	

Cook pasta according to directions. In large bowl whisk oil, mustard, pesto, and pepper. Add vegetables and chives. Stir in hot pasta with vegetable mixture and add Parmesan and basil. Serve immediately.

Tip: If you have garden cherry tomatoes, you will need about a cup. A couple quartered green or yellow tomatoes tossed in look (and taste) very appealing.

Three-Grain Rice with Lentils

2 cups	water
1 cup	organic vegetable broth
1 cup	brown rice
3/4 cup	wild rice
1/4 cup	barley
1/4 cup	lentils
1	carrot, chopped in small pieces
1/2 tsp	dried chives
6–7	leaves of spinach

Take a large pot and fill with 2 cups of water and 1 cup of vegetable broth. Put in wild rice and brown rice. Cook on medium heat for 20 minutes. Add barley, lentils, carrot and chives. Cook until rice is well cooked (wild rice should be opened) which should be another 25 minutes. Throw in spinach leaves for last 2 minutes of cooking.

Doubling the recipe is recommended as it makes a side dish for 3–4 meals. Add other ingredients such as garlic, Swiss chard, cooked chicken cubes, black beans, green or red pepper for extra nutrients and flavoring. This is a good starter to get creative with.

Wild Rice & Chickpea Salad

1 cup	wild rice
1 can	chickpeas, drained
1 can	black beans, drained
1 can	niblets corn, drained
1/2 cup	chopped red pepper
1/2 cup	chopped purple onion

Dressing:

3 tbsp	lemon juice, freshly squeezed
1/8 cup	olive oil
2 tsp	dried or fresh oregano or basil
1 tbsp	white vinegar or balsamic vinegar

Cook wild rice for 40–45 minutes and drain. Let cool or run cold water through and drain again. Add remaining ingredients. Mix dressing and pour over salad. Serve cold on lettuce leaves.

Wild Rice Chicken Skillet

1 1/2 cups	wild rice
1 can	low-sodium stewed tomatoes
2 tbsp	olive oil
1 can	white beans
1 lb	chicken breasts cut in chunks
1 tsp	basil or thyme
2 tsp	minced garlic
1/2 cup	chopped red peppers
2 cups	frozen or fresh broccoli florets

Cook wild rice for 40–45 minutes and drain. In large skillet, cook chicken pieces in olive oil until brown. Add chopped red pepper and garlic and sauté until tender. Add stewed tomatoes, beans, herbs and broccoli and cook for 5–7 minutes stirring occasionally. Mix with wild rice and serve. Double the recipe and use leftovers as a soup by adding vegetable broth or tomato soup. Also good in a whole-wheat wrap with a little cheese.

Yogurt Pancakes

1 3/4 cups	whole-wheat flour
1/4 cup	ground flax meal
1 tbsp	chia (*ground*)
2 tsp	baking powder
2	beaten eggs
1 packet	Stevia
2 tbsp	sunflower oil
1 cup	fruit yogurt of any flavor (*watch sugar content*)

Almond milk (*as desired consistency*)
Optional: add blueberries

Mix dry ingredients in large bowl. Add rest of the ingredients to the dry mix in bowl and add cup of milk. Keep adding milk to mixture until it is a smooth semi-thick consistency. Heat pan with 1 tbsp of oil. Spoon in pancake mix and cook at low heat until golden brown and cooked throughout. Makes enough for 4 people.

Your Victory Journal

This space is for you to capture your ideas, insights and plans toward the implementation of better health and well being. Your journey is unique, so personalize this as much as you desire. No one is grading or measuring you. Be open to possibilities and focus on the process, not the end result.

Recommended readings

Aamondt, S., & Wang, S. (2008). Welcome to your brain, why you lose your car keys and never forget how to drive and other Puzzles of everyday life. New York: Bloomsbury.

Balch, P. (2008). Prescription for nutritional healing, the A to Z guide to supplements. New York: Penguin.

Barnard, N.D. (2007 Dr. Neal Barnard's program for reversing diabetes. New York: Rosdale Books

Bitman, M. (2009). Food Matters. New York: Simon & Schuster.

Braverman, E.R. (2009) Younger (thinner) you diet. New York: Rosdale Books.

Cabot, S. (1996). The liver-cleansing diet, love your liver and live longer. Scottsdale: S.C.B. International.

Carper, J. (2000). You miracle brain, maximize your brain power, boost your memory, lift your mood, improve your IQ and creativity, prevent and reverse mental aging.

Cheung, L. & Hanh, T.N. (2010). Savor: Mindful eating, mindful life. New York: Harper One.

Chopra, D., & Simon, D. (2001). Grow younger, live longer, 10 steps to reverse aging. New York: Three Rivers Press.

Dean, C. (2007). The magnesium miracle. New York: Ballantine

DeMaria, R. (2005). Dr. Bob's guide to stop ADHD in 18 days. Elyria, OH: Drugless Health Solutions.

Feldon, L., & Greene, R.A. (2005). Dr. Robert Greene's perfect balance. New York: Three Rivers Press.

Fitzgerald, R. (2006). The Hundred-Year Lie. New York: Dutton.

Frusztajer, Marquis, N., & Wurtman, J.J. (2006). The serotonin power diet. New York: Rodale Books.

Hart, A., (1991). Adrenalin and Stress: The Exciting New Breakthrough That Helps You Overcome Stress Damage. Dallas: Word Publishing.

Heller, F., (Rachael), & Heller, F., (Richard) (2010). The stress eating cure. New York: Rodale Books.

Hyman, M. (2009) The ultramind solution. New York: Scribner.

Johnson, R.J. (with Gower, T.) (2008). The sugar fix. New York: Pocket Books.

Katz, D. (2005). The flavor point: The delicious breakthrough plan to turn off your hunger and lose the weight for good. New York: Rodale.

Kessler, D.A. (2009). The end of overeating. Taking control of the insatiable North American appetite. Toronto: McClelland & Stewart.

Kleiner, S., (with Condor, B.) (2007). The good mood diet: Feel great while you lose weight. New York: Springboard Press.

Lawlis, F. (2009). Retraining the brain: A 45-day plan to conquer stress and anxiety. New York: Plume.

Murray, M. (1998). Boost your serotonin levels, 5-HTP: The natural way to overcome depression, obesity and insomnia. New York: Bantam.

Patterson, K., & Grenney, J., & Maxfield, D., & McMillan, R., & Switzler, A. (2008). The influencer: The power to change anything. New York: McGraw-Hill.

Perricone, N. (2002). The perricone prescription. New York: HarperCollins.

Prevention Magazine Editors (with Fittante, A.) (2006). Prevention's: The sugar solution. New York: Rosdale Books.

Ross, J. (2002). The mood cure. New York: Pengquin Books.

Schlosser, E. (2001). Fast food nation: The dark side of the all-american meal. New York: First Mariner

Somer, E. (1999). Food & mood: The complete guide to eating well and feeling your best. New York: Holt Paperbacks.

Tabott, S. (2004). The cortisol connection diet: The breakthrough program to control stress and lose weight. Alameda: Hunter House.

Turner, N. (2009). The hormone diet: Lose fat, gain strength and live longer. Toronto: Random House.

Waterhouse, D. (1995). Why women need chocolate. Scranton: Hyperion.

Weil, A. (1997). 8 weeks to optimum health. New York: Ballantine.

Winner, J. (2003). Take the stress out of your life. New York: Da Capo Press.

About the author

Treena Wynes is a Registered Social Worker and owner of *Food4Thought* Counselling Service in Saskatoon, Saskatchewan, Canada. She is an active speaker, workshop host, blogger and food activist. She is married to a social worker and has two boys ages 18 and 15. Their favorite family activity is downhill skiing in British Columbia.

Treena hopes this book will influence her readers to take a look at their current diets and empower them to make two or three positive changes that will enhance their quality of life. She also hopes it compels her readers to further investigate how to be proactive in maintaining health and fighting illness in a society that does not promote holistic health or natural solutions.

She would like to thank all her circle of supporters and those who challenge her and motivate her to seek more knowledge.

www.eatingmyselfcrazy.com

Other Indie Ink books you might enjoy

indie ink
PUBLISHING

Blown Away:
A year through the lens of The Tornado Hunter
By Greg Johnson

Hardcover $34.95 CAD $29.95 USD
ISBN 978-0-9878105-1-9

One man's journey into and through one of the most horrific and awe-inspiring storm seasons on record. Join Canada's Tornado Hunter, Greg Johnson, on this deeply personal journey and you, too, will be Blown Away.

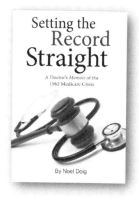

Setting the Record Straight:
A doctor's memoir of the 1962 Medicare crisis
by Noel Doig

Hardcover $29.95 CAD $24.95 USD
ISBN: 978-0-9878105-3-3

Most people know that in 1962, Saskatchewan became the "birthplace of Medicare," and that the rest of Canada soon followed. However, few people today remember the political fight that the people of Saskatchewan and its doctors waged in opposition to their government's Plan. In the 50th anniversary year of Saskatchewan's Medical Care Insurance Act, Dr. Noel Doig presents for the first time what the introduction of Medicare meant from the perspective of the doctors and patients of Saskatchewan at the time. With rich storytelling detail, and punctuated by the witty political cartoons of the late Saskatoon Star Phoenix/Regina Leader Post artist Ed Sebestyen, Doig recounts in dramatic fashion the story of how politics trumped principle.

Other Indie Ink books you might enjoy

indie ink
PUBLISHING

**The New Rockstar Philosophy:
a guerrilla blueprint for digitally conscious artists**
by Matt Voyno & Roshan Hoover

Softcover $19.95 CAD $15.95 USD
ISBN 978-0-9878105-8-8

Hailed by indie musician-composer Michael Franti as "an outstanding guide for the Internet-era D.I.Y. musician who wants to thrive in today's post-major label music industry," the updated guide promises to be a "guerrilla blueprint for digitally conscious artists." Festival organizers, band managers, musicians, digital devotees and co-authors Matt Voyno and Roshan Hoover bring their award winning e-book to paper book format. From budding musician to road tested journeyman; from songwriter to band leader to publicist to producer—all will get value from the straight talk on how to build your brand from the ground up in the digital age.

Fiction

Strange Places (Book One of *Finding Tayna*)
by Jefferson Smith

Softcover $22.95 CAD $14.95 USD
ISBN: 978-0-9866936-1-8

If you liked Katniss, you'll love Tayna. If you enjoyed the thrills of Harry Potter, grab this first fantasy in the Finding Tayna series. Tayna is every villain's worst nightmare: an uncooperative victim who refuses to play by his rules. When Lord Angiron arrives at the run-down city orphanage, ready to "rescue" her from a life of slavery, Tayna learns that she may never have actually been an orphan and flees to find her family. But time is running out, and this feisty teen must search two strange worlds: one filled with shopping malls and TVs, and another filled with Brownies, Djin and magic.

To learn where to purchase these books, or to find out more about Indie Ink, visit us at indieinkpublishing.com. And don't forget to like us on Facebook!